After qualifying from Edinburgh University in 1941, Dr. Walter Yellowless served in World War II as a RAMC officer; in 1948 he joined Dr. Jack Swanson in the Aberfeldy practice; there, he and his wife, Sonia Doggart brought up their family of two boys and a girl.

Lady Eve Balfour's book, *The Living Soil*, guided Walter to the researches of Sir Robert McCarrison who had proved, beyond doubt, the truth that sound nutrition was the basis of human health. As a lecturer and author of the book *A Doctor in the Wilderness*, Dr. Yellowless has tried to spread the virtues of the Organic Movement. Now aged 91, in his book, *A Time to Weep*, he looks back to growing up in rural Renfrewshire and deplores our departure from the Christian faith as the cause of rising crime, drug and alcohol addiction and family breakdown. He is a long-standing Elder of Aberfeldy Church in Scotland.

A TIME TO WEEP

Dr. Walter W. Yellowlees. MC, MB ChB, FRCGP

A TIME TO WEEP

Watty Yellowlees

Sue Pheasant

AUSTIN & MACAULEY

A CIP catalogue record for this title is available from the British Library.

ISBN 978 1 905609 66-6

www.austinmacauley.com

First Published (2009)
Austin & Macauley Publishers Ltd.
25 Canada Square
Canary Wharf
London
E14 5LB

Printed & Bound in Great Britain

This book is dedicated to the memory of my dear wife, Sonia. Without her devotion and help during my years in the Aberfeldy General Medical Practice, I doubt if I could have survived the stresses of the job, especially in those early years when a GP's wife had to be a telephonist and part-time receptionist.

CONTENTS

FOREWORD

By the Reverend Sandy Gunn MA BD, former Church of Scotland minister of St. Andrews and Thrumster parishes, Wick; St.Davids, Knightswood, Glasgow and Aberfeldy, Amulree and Weem, Perthshire.

Diagnosis is the key! Imagine a doctor noticing some spots on a patient, sometimes in uncomfortable places. While alleviating some symptoms might be of some help, it would be a poor doctor who would not see beyond the individual spots to the underlying cause – chickenpox, measles etc.

While there are some people who try to alleviate some of the individual "spots of trouble" in our world, there are few who realise that these issues are only symptoms of an underlying disease, and even fewer who have made the diagnosis, often affecting uncomfortable places, commenting on which is not "politically correct".

Dr. Yellowlees is one of these! An original thinker working from evidence and first principles his previous book, "A Doctor in the Wilderness", combined research-based argument and human interest anecdote to challenge fearlessly both individuals and governments about the role of diet in the cause of preventive illness. This "healthy eating" approach is taken further in "A Time to Weep" as it looks at some worrying trends in society. As we need healthy food for our bodies so we need healthy food for our minds – truth without which we suffer mental/spiritual malnutrition!

Too often present-day thinking is compartmentalised, and the Christian faith, if considered at all, is relegated – to be charitable perhaps subconsciously – by vested interests to the third division as a placebo hobby of a pious few, replacing it with image, feelings, and the illusion of instant success. However, this alert doctor diagnoses the underlying cause of the trouble "spots" of global society and personal living as the decline in the Christian faith, the historic message of Jesus Christ as truth belonging to the public arena. A compartmentalising mentality may try to stress other factors, but when evidence from all aspects is collated and ethical consequence of abandonment of the truth of the Christian faith emerges clearly as the ultimate diagnosis.

Academic research often appears dry and unfeeling. The very title of "A Time to Weep" underlines the depth not only of understanding, but also of caring which comes across in the pages of this book. Given the evidence that Jesus is both the "Truth" and "Love" then integrity of thought and depth of care will be combined in the lives of His followers. These are embodied in Dr. Yellowlees, as I can vouch from my own knowledge of him over many years. I therefore gladly commend the challenge of this book and its awareness of the underlying issues facing our world as a template for thinking, caring people.

ACKNOWLEDGEMENTS

Firstly, I give thanks to all those friends who have encouraged me in this attempt to write a second book. I am particularly grateful to our former, and recently retired Church of Scotland minister, the Reverend Sandy Gunn, for his advice on the interpretation of certain Biblical passages, and for his agreement to write the Foreword for *A Time to Weep*.

A writer who, in old age, seeks to defend the Christian faith inevitably looks back with gratitude to the origins of his own beliefs: – parents, and grandparents, the school chaplain at Merchiston Castle School, the Rev. W.M. Laing, who, in the nineteen thirties guided senior pupils in taking their first communion. Then, in the nineteen forties, the example of the Rev. Coty Smith, Padre of the 5th Battallion of the Cameron Highlanders, a shining light of Christian faith and courage amidst the shot and shell of battle, in World War 2. Nearer home I must thank the Rev. Eddi.e. Lowe, minister in Aberfeldy during the 1960s who, by his persuasion, overcame my reluctance to become an elder of our church.

There is no space here to name all the fellow elders and members of the congregation whose friendship through the years has sustained my faith; a special word of thanks goes to our Church Reader, Gregor McMartin for his example and for his contributions to our bible study group.

Ian Menzies, Aberfeldy Church of Scotland's former skilful music technician, electronic expert, and Church Newsletter publisher, created the graph of Crimes and Offences based on the figures sent by the Scottish Office Home Department; he also helped to prepare the other illustrations for inclusion in the text.

I thank John McDiarmid of Mains of Murthly Farm, Aberfeldy, who took the evocative photographs of the inscribed stone, placed on Strachurmore Farm Hill Park, in memory of my brother Robin; and I repeat my thanks, expressed in chapter 4, to Catherine and Tom Paton, of Leachd, Strathlachlan for saving the stone from damage due to the attention of grazing sheep and cattle.

In recent years, during my annual visits to Strachur in order to inspect the stone, I have received wonderful support from the warm B&B hospitality of Rob and Sheila McPherson, the Old Manse,

Strachur. The comfort, delicious meals, and entertaining conversation at the Old Manse gave a good base for me to indulge in memories of the 1930s at Strachurmore – a time of youth, of hard farm work and hilarity, a time full of dreams of our future – dreams which, in September 1939, were shattered when Hitler's tanks rolled into Poland.

A consultant physician once warned me that hospital doctors, in doing a daily ward round, become familiar with the appearance of long term patients. Through that very familiarity, they may miss the gradual changes which signal a specific disease, such as thyroid gland deficiency. It was therefore wise, he advised, to arrange a visit by an outside observer who might immediately recognise the signs a specific disease.

The same phenomenon certainly applies to my writing; I always asked my late wife, Sonia, to scan important letters or documents which I had written and was often appalled at the glaring mistakes which she had found and I had missed. I sometimes wonder if I have inherited a touch of dyslexia! I am therefore grateful to have had the advice of the following two proof readers:

Mrs Sue Pheasant who lives in the south of England, whom I have not had the pleasure of meeting, has given to me valuable references to the evidence of the forces of darkness, such as the hate-filled writings of the Humanist Society, which, in the past and still today, seek to destroy our Christian faith. She has also given sound corrections on punctuation and on the lay-out of paragraphs.

The late Mr Ian Grant, worked for many years as Aberfeldy's dentist. Until his sad death in 2001, he was my friend and colleague, on the golf course, in his dental surgery, where I often administered anaesthetics; and as a fellow church elder. Ian held strong views on the caring professions and on the affairs of church and state. He served for many years on Aberfeldy Town Council (Before idiotic politicians abolished rural town councils with their Provosts) His widow, Penny, a close friend of Sonia, now teaches English as a part-time tutor, has read the script of *A Time to Weep*. I am deeply grateful to these two ladies for their valuable comments and corrections.

A TIME TO WEEP

INTRODUCTION

Remember now thy creator in the days of thy youth
while the evil days come not, nor the days draw nigh
when thou shalt say I have no pleasure in them...
In the days when the keepers of the house shall tremble
and the strong men shall bow themselves and the grinders
cease because they are few, and those that look out of the
windows be darkened

(Ecclesiastes chap. 12)

In contemplating old age, the author of the Book of Ecclesiastes writes as a sceptic and a pessimist. The above verses of chapter 12 are followed by a long list of the bodily infirmities which plague the elderly. The pains, frustration, fatigue and discomfort of failing bodily functions are expressed in vivid poetic images – *the keepers of the house* are the arms and hands; they often *tremble* in old age. The *strong men shall bow themselves* is a picture of "bowed" osteoarthritic joints of the legs or the bending of the back; the *grinders* are our crumbling molar teeth, (in modern times, usually replaced by a set of dentures!); *windows be darkened* tells of failing vision. (6)

Few of us, as we pass into our eighties, can claim to be free from these infirmities, but surely many of us, as we live out our sunset days, need not cry that *we have no pleasure in them.* There are compensations. When advancing age compels the player of energetic ball games to retire to the touch line or grandstand as a spectator, he or she often has the great satisfaction of seeing much more of the contest than they did in the days of vigorous youth, days when, on the field of play, they were caught up in the heat and fury of the match. So it is with the game of life. As we age, emotion becomes tempered by experience. The dictates of adrenalin – the hormone which triggers fight or flight – give place to some measure of serenity.

As I try to explain why this year 2005 is *A Time to Weep* I am sure that younger readers will simply write me off as a typical example of the senile grumbler who lives in a past golden age that never was, and who deplores all things new. Yes, memory is mercifully selective and, as we look back, it tends to favour pleasant things and to shut away painful ones. But is it not the duty of those who live long and who are convinced of terrible dangers which lie ahead, to give warning of catastrophe?

If I sound like an Old Testament prophet so be it; our nation now faces spiritual and physical dangers not unlike those which threatened Israel and Judah some eight hundred years before the coming of Christ. The Hebrew tribe's leaders had failed to uphold the divine law. Unchecked, they had turned against their true God; they had gone after the idols of neighbouring tribes and indulged in drunken orgies, sexual rites, prostitution and child-sacrifice (Isaiah Ch 57) ; the prophets of Israel warned of the terrible punishment which awaited God's chosen people:

> *Hear this …you rulers of the house of Israel who despise justice and distort all that is right; who build Zion with bloodshed and Jerusalem with wickedness; …her leaders judge for a bribe; her priests teach for a price, and her prophets tell fortunes for money…Therefore because of you Jerusalem will become a heap of rubble.*

Thus the prophet Micah (Ch.3:8-12) spoke out against the oppression, corruption and decadence of the rulers of Israel and Judah. He foretold the conquest and destruction of the ten northern tribes by Assyria and the later destruction of Judah. Is this not an uncomfortable reminder of what has happened and what is happening today in Britain's godless permissive society? Again, I quote from Ecclesiastes:

What has been will be again, what has been done will be done again; there is nothing new under the sun. (chap 1, v. 9). The rise and fall of nation after nation during the span of recorded history, certainly confirms this sad conclusion. The fall of nations and empires was invariably associated with the corruption of their leaders who abandoned spiritual truths and the welfare of their subjects;

they pursued personal wealth, luxury and sexual immorality, family life disintegrated; crimes of violence increased:

> *Leaders ceased to be statesmen and became politicians, bribing, lying and intriguing in pursuit of their private interests* (1)

In the centuries before the birth of Jesus the kingdom of Israel had split into two conflicting factions, ten tribes in the north, known as Israel, and to the south, the tribes of Judah and Benjamin holding the small area round Jerusalem. Around 700 BC, Israel was over-run by the Assyrians and disappeared as a Jewish entity; Judah survived conquest and Babylonian captivity and by the time of the birth of Jesus the small enclave of land around Jerusalem had become part of the Roman Empire. Scribes and Pharisees ruled over Judah; they had imposed ever more detailed elaboration of the law; the Ten Commandments became six hundred and thirteen; directives were contrived for all possible eventualities (2); (compare this with the output of present day Brussels' bureaucrats; *there is nothing new under the sun)* Pharisaic dictatorship continued to impose and to profit from the rituals of animal sacrifice; their leaders eagerly expected the coming of the promised Messiah who would proclaim the superiority of God's chosen race and would lead the armies of Zion to destroy and enslave all other nations. (Deuteronomy chap. 20)

The young carpenter from Gallilee fearlessly condemned this philosophy; he exposed the hypocrisy and corruption of the Pharisees and preached the way of love and peace; the Kingdom of Heaven would not come by Jewish racial superiority through widespread slaughter and military conquest. Jesus well knew that his opposition to the Pharisaic rule would inevitably lead to the Cross. As he paused on the Mount of Olives, on his way to that fateful Passover celebration, and gazed at the city of Jerusalem he wept because he foreknew that the policy of violence and rebellion against the Roman authorities, rather than the way of peace, would result in disaster: (Luke Ch 19: 41-44).

In AD 70 the Romans, exasperated at the threat of Jewish insurrection, did indeed, totally destroy Jerusalem.

When, having paused on the Mount of Olives, Jesus entered Jerusalem and arrived at the temple his moment of weeping turned to fury; the *Time to Weep*, according to Luke, gave way to a time to act, he threw over the tables of priestly officials who were using the Passover to enrich themselves at the expense of unfortunate pilgrims. The racketeers, repeating the sins of their Old Testament predecessors, fled from the wrath of Jesus.

As my generation read our daily newspapers or watch TV news, we surely can be forgiven if we are often inwardly moved to weep; we feel powerless to do anything about the violence, depravity and lawlessness of modern Britain.

This book is my attempt to act; but how dare a retired GP, lacking scholastic background, venture on such a task? As I pondered and hesitated, certain things spurred me to put pen to paper. I chanced to read that according to statistics issued in 1995 by the Scottish Office Home Department, crimes and offences cleared up by the police in 1940 numbered 182,543; by 1994 the number had risen to 637,946. Various factors – changes in legislation, classification of crimes, changes in population and so on – may question whether the increase in crime is real. But daily experience can often give a more compelling picture than statistics.

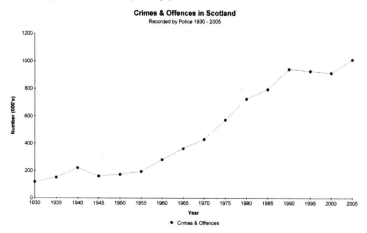

Crimes & Offences in Scotland
Recorded by Police 1930 - 2005

Here are three instances:

1). My daughter works in Edinburgh; her car, parked in the street below her flat is repeatedly subjected to minor acts of vandalism; it was stolen the other day and found, a few weeks later, in a distant suburb.

2). Some years ago, after an evening meeting at Edinburgh University staff club I 'phoned to my son who lived on the other side of a near-by public park ("The Meadows"); I had been invited to stay for the night and I simply wanted to let him and his wife know that I was on my way and would walk along the footpath by The Meadows. He said that on no account should I walk because unsavoury characters were known to lurk there after nightfall. Their mugging and robbery supply the cash to sustain their drug addiction.

3). The scene enacted during every school term lunch-time on Aberfeldy's streets and, I dare say, on the streets of any other township having in its midst a Primary and Senior school:

The pavements are thronged with a flood of noisy, disreputable, disorderly pupils; they pay little heed to any one in their way and crowd out the entrances of food and confectionary shops; they eat their lunch on the pavements or any public space, often scattering food debris.

Here are my comments on these three instances:

INSTANCE 1

I mention the missing car simply because theft, burglary and shop-lifting seem to be an accepted feature of life today. The scale of thieving is infinitely greater now than in the first half of the 20th century.

INSTANCE 2

This gives evidence of the terrible prevalence of the drug culture which spawns violent theft, gang warfare and sometimes murder. In the 1930s during my undergraduate years at Edinburgh University drug addiction did not appear in the medical curriculum. Then it was known as a very rare occurrence; Douglas Guthrie's *History of Medicine* published in 1945 makes no mention of drug addiction; but now the 1991 edition of a popular text book of medicine (3) states that since 1970 drug addiction in Western countries has become a major problem. *In the United Kingdom there are now 50,000 – 100,000 opiate addicts and 2% of the population regularly take benzodiazipam* – to say nothing of cannabis. Why has this come about? How have we allowed this epidemic to destroy thousands of lives and to cause elderly residents in our cities to be terrified to go out after dark? Between 1936 and 1941 I often visited friends who lived in one of the flats overlooking The Meadows. Never, in those days, was there any mention of, or fear of, mugging.

INSTANCE 3

I suppose that in today's permissive climate it is too much to expect education authorities and parents to insist on pupils sitting down for a school lunch of fresh food prepared by friendly cooks. Joining others at meal times is an important aspect of civilisation; and do education authorities not know of the research which blames the consumption of highly processed, artificially coloured and sweetened foods and drinks, as the cause of disturbed behaviour in children? (4) It is good to know that recently Jami.e. Oliver's TV programme highlights this problem.

In my book, *A doctor in the Wilderness,* I sought to explain how the dreadful state of Scotland's bodily health is caused by a totally inadequate diet and how our health might, by simple dietary reform, be restored. The following chapters attempt to set out an old man's views on the decline of our spiritual health. Spiritual and physical health are linked and although, in both cases, mechanisms are infinitely complex, basic causes are simple.

The problems of law and order, family breakdown, chaos in schools, failures in the Health Service, corruption in trade and politics are endlessly featured in the media. But none of the pundits seem inclined to admit the possibility of the simple cause which is at the heart of our troubles – it is that we are no longer a Christian nation.

To quote from the writings of the late William Barclay, distinguished Greek scholar, author, University lecturer and Church of Scotland parish minister, whose prolific writings, especially his commentaries on the New Testament have strengthened the faith of countless readers:

> *The care of the sick, the aged and the poor began as a Christian undertaking.*
>
> *There was no such thing as a hospital til Christianity came. Aristotle, in laying down the laws for his ideal state says, ' Let there be a law that no deformed child shall be reared'. Varro, in giving rules for farming, advises that any aged slave who is past his work should be thrown out and left to die, just as a broken farm implement is thrown on to the rubbish heap.*
>
> *If the Christian ethic is removed, all that is good in the welfare state will be removed too....Let those who wish to enjoy the privileges of a Christian country remember that they will not enjoy them long if the country ceases to be Christian...Freedom of speech and conscience are specifically Christian possessions.*
>
> *Those who wish to enjoy all the privileges of a Christian civilisation ought to ask themselves if they are doing anything to keep civilisation Christian; and if they are not, they will have no one but themselves to blame if they wake up some day to find their privileges gone. (5)*

Chapters 1 and 2 are an attempt to give the reader a glimpse of my family background which I hope will explain the origins of my theme. I hasten to reassure that I have no wish at all to write an autobiography but I hope that an account of the climate of thought and behaviour in the days of my youth will help the reader to understand why I believe now is *A time to Weep* and a time for action.

REFERENCES

1. Glubb, Sir J.B. *The Way of Love* Hodder and Stoughton, 1973, London.
2. Source Book of the Bible. SCM Press, 1970.
3. Davidson's *Principles and Practice of Medicine* Churchill, Livingston 1991.
4. Menzies Ian C. *Disturbed and Disturbing Children – The Role of Diet and the Dietician in Child Psychiatry. 1985,* Lecture to McCarrison Society.
5. Barclay. *Through the Year with William Barclay.* p149 Hodder and Stoughton 1971
6. Pepper, O.H.P (1952) Am.J.med. Sci, 223, 589

CHAPTER 1
CARPETS, WELFARE AND LAND USE

In 1918 the Caledonian Carpet Company of Stirling, under the management of my father, David Yellowlees, merged with two other Scottish carpet manufacturing firms, A.F. Stoddards Ltd, of Elderslie, and Paisley's Ronald Jack & Co. With management centred at Elderslie, David Yellowlees and Stuart Jack became joint Managing Directors of the new unified company.

So in 1919 my father with his wife, Mary Primrose, Robin aged 5 and me, aged 2, moved from Stirling to Glenpatrick House, Elderslie where my brother David was born two years later.

The garden of our new home sloped down to a lovely wooded gorge through which ran a swift-flowing burn; because of its amber peaty colour, it was named the "Brandy Burn". In 1815 three dams had been built to serve the paper mill working at the lower end of the Glenpatrick gorge. After some 15 years the paper mill failed, as did the company which took over the mill to manufacture, first Paisley shawls, then tapestry carpets; in 1862 the company was declared bankrupt.

However, up stream from the mill, since 1834 the dams had been used to establish the Gleniffer Whisky Distillery. A few moss-covered remains of stone and brick walls by the water falls mark the sites of warehouses, cart sheds, stills and work shops. Before it closed, probably around 1890, the distillery's annual output is recorded as 70,000 gallons of pure malt. My sketch on page 44 shows, beside the waterfall, the remnant of a stone wall of one of the distillery buildings

ENTER ARTHUR STODDARD

Let us return to the lower mill, bankrupt in 1862 after failing to sell enough carpets.

At that time, an American business man, Arthur Stoddard had established a branch of his export business in Glasgow. He had come to Scotland from Northampton, Massachusetts, probably because he opposed slavery and supported the Northern faction in the American Civil War; he seems to have been a man of great energy and enterprise; within five years of taking over the failed Glenpatrick factory, three quarters of its output of carpets were being exported to America.

In 1881, such was the success of the now greatly enlarged factory, that Arthur Stoddard was able to preside at a ceremony in the village of Eldersli.e. (birth place of Scotland's hero, William Wallace), to open a public hall and reading room, built at his own expense. In reporting the event, the Paisley Daily Express of 20th August 1881 quoted Arthur Stoddard's speech as follows:

Soon after I became proprietor of the Glenpatrick carpet works I resolved, if God prospered the undertaking and my life was spared, that I would testify my gratitude to the Giver of all Good, and as a recognition of my work people and those connected with them, by providing a reading room and a library for their benefit. I lost no time in formulating this purpose in my will if I should not live to carry out the plan myself. I felt it was my duty to interest myself in the moral, social, cultural and religious welfare of my work people. In these respects I have left undone many of the things which I ought to have done, yet I recognise my responsibilities, and trust my shortcomings in time past will be somewhat atoned for by what I have lived to see completed… Had I been the proprietor of land about here, or had it been possible to acquire it, I should have been disposed to lay off a few acres and to build for my work people neat and commodious houses, each one separated from the other, with well laid out grounds and garden plots adorned with flowers, where every man could sit, if not under his own vine or fig tree, at least under his own porch or apple tree, and feel he was lord of all he surveyed.

Those of you who remember that stuffy little weaving shed with its 24 looms will feel a sort of family pride in its contrast with the present shed, where about a hundred and twenty are now beating time to the music of better wages and steady pay.

These sentiments, laced with biblical references, uttered more than a hundred years ago will no doubt be dismissed by today's predominately atheist readers as pretentious, sanctimonious, quaint and irrelevant. But although described as a vigorous, determined, correct and domineering man, Arthur Stoddard was surely a sincere Christian who "identified himself with the community among whom he settled"; his vision of a time when a worker could sit, *if not under his own vine or fig tree at least under his own porch or apple tree* is taken from the words of our friend, the prophet Micah, quoted in my introduction. Micah's strictures, echoing Stoddard's views, were aimed at Jerusalem's wealthy, corrupt landowners in the years between 740 and 715 BC:

They covet fields and seize them, and houses and take them. They defraud a man of his home and a fellow man of his inheritance (Micah, Ch2:2). These words might well apply to the Highland Clearances and to aspects of our industrial revolution which brought about rural depopulation, decline in our agriculture and the creation of vast conurbations with their dreadful slums.

TOWN AND COUNTRY HOUSES

The warnings of Micah and Isaiah – they both worked during the same time in history – could apply exactly to our unwise use of land today: *Woe to you who add house to house and join field to field 'til no space is left, and you live alone in the land (Isaiah 5: 8)* Was Arthur Stoddard echoing these words when he spoke of his hope to create for his workers *commodious houses each one separated from the other with well lain out grounds and garden plots?* Houses being built today defy this teaching; we are adding "house to house" with no garden between even in rural areas. What would Micah and Isaiah think of our tower blocks where *house on top of house* separates families from the green-growing earth? It will certainly be *A Time to Weep* if, following some catastrophe in the Middle East or elsewhere, we will have no oil for the transport of our food from foreign farms, and no gardens nor fields to grow our own.

Arthur Stoddard died in the year following the opening of Elderslie's Reading Room.

The company continued to prosper and expand under the Chairmanship of his son-in-law, Sir Charles Renshaw Bt.

TOILETS AND BATHROOMS

I do not know if the high priority given by Arthur Stoddard to the welfare of his employees and of the surrounding community was typical of Scotland's industries in the late nineteenth and early 20th centuries. However, my father and Stewart Jack, as joint Managing Directors of the new merged company, in 1919 certainly faced the urgent need to upgrade the flats and houses occupied by their work force. Father often told of his dismay at finding the inadequate plumbing and ghastly dry privies. An extensive building programme soon installed new bathrooms and flush toilets.

One block of flats stood over the fence from our garden; Peter Donald, a boy of about my age, whose family occupied a ground floor flat became a great pal. Mrs Gallacher, a widow, lived in an upstairs flat, and every Sunday one of us would take to her a generous helping of our Sunday lunch, always roast beef and roast potatoes.

Jimmy Bolton drove the works lorry, a vehicle with brass radiator and large brass headlamps; the memory of the latter has not faded; one summer's day, while larking and bicycle-racing with friends, head down, peddling as fast as possible, I collided with the lorry's head lamps and still bear the scar of the wound on my right cheek.

After the upgrading of the firm's houses, a works canteen was opened in 1920 and in 1924 came the founding of the Stoddard Provident Society which gave employees who wished to join, a savings fund for retirement. The scheme seems to have been very popular; to mark its inauguration the employees presented to the Directors an inkstand, inscribed: *Presented to the Board of Directors of Messrs A.F. Stoddard & Co Ltd. by their employees at their Glenpatrick Works, to mark the inauguration of the Stoddard Provident Society. 1st October 1924.*

Good Relationships

My recollection of those days in the Glenpatrick works is of a climate of trust and friendliness, almost a family feeling between management and workers. I hope that my memory does not fail me when I write that disputes between labour and management did not occur. During the 27 years of our life at Glenpatrick House, in spite of the trade depression of the thirties, trust and friendship seemed to survive.

This history of the 1920s at the Glenpatrick factory is in sharp contrast with the unrest elsewhere in the industrial cities of Europe. In the aftermath of World War One, unemployment, hunger, and monetary inflation led to widespread discontent among workers, many of whom were ex-soldiers hoping for "a land fit for heroes." In the Russian revolution of 1917, Lenin's Godless Marxist regime, with its gospel of State control, hatred, terrorism and class warfare had seized power. Industrial unrest in Britain so alarmed the government that in 1921 plans were made ready to deploy troops in London.(1) During the 27 years of our family life at Glenpatrick, in spite of the vicissitudes of trade and politics, trust and friendship seemed to survive.

Far-flung Trade Links

My father used his unique ability to make friends and establish trust to the benefit of Stoddard's trade. He went on several long journeys to the firm's agencies all over the world; air travel was, of course, then undreamed of; voyages by sea to Australia, New Zealand, Canada, the Middle East and the Americas took him from home for many months at a time, almost a year for one voyage. The people he met in the course of these travels remained staunch friends some of whom continued to visit my parents even after my father retired.

I do not know how much father's energetic travelling to overseas agents enabled Stoddards to weather the 1930s trade depression, but I am sure that it was the enterprise of the management team under the chairmanship of Sir Stephen Renshaw (who had succeeded his father Sir Charles) which kept the firm afloat in difficult times.

Overseas agents and buyers often came to visit the factory; they lunched at Glenpatrick House, some times at short notice, so that mother would be hard put to it to produce an appetising meal; invariably she did! During school holidays we children sat as (mostly silent) helpers at these meals; the talk among the adults often dwelt on the problems of cheap carpets, imported from countries where labour costs were much lower than in the UK.

TRIUMPH AND DISASTER

Hitler's war interrupted carpet manufacturing at Stoddards; in 1939 the factory switched to the production of life jackets and other necessities of war. After the war, in 1946 my father, by then aged 73, retired. He and my mother moved to a cottage on the outskirts of Perth.

By 1962 the firm, now expanded to The Stoddard Group or Stoddard International, had become one of the largest carpet manufacturers in Europe; in May of that year in a banqueting hall in Paisley, A.F. Stoddard & Co Ltd. celebrated the firm's centenary; gold watches were presented to long-serving employees and Premium Bonds to other employees according to length of service.

The transformation from a shed with its water mill, driven by the Brandy Burn, is surely a triumph of humane capitalism. *Large streams from little fountains flow/ Tall oaks from little acorns grow.*

That paragraph was mostly written in 1993/4 before the ending of what seems to have been a long and happy history. I do not know why one of Europe's largest and most successful carpet manufacturers came to grief.

Following trade losses of over £900,000, in 2002 Stoddard International was relocated at Kilmarnock with the loss of about 100 jobs; the Eldersli.e. site was sold to a Scottish builder (the Walker Group) for between £7 and £10 million. Now, in 2005, the factory has been partly demolished for house building. In spite of strong objections from the people of Elderslie, permission has been given for the building of 126 homes on and around the cleared factory site. I am grateful to Miss Agnes Barr, now aged 95 and still going strong, who, in the 1920s and 30s, worked as a secretary/typist in my father's office, for sending to me press cuttings which featured recent developments at the Eldersli.e. factory.

Does the sad ending of Stoddards confirm the late A.F Schumacher's dictum that "Small is Beautiful"? Perhaps this development is all to the good in meeting the apparently increasing demand for houses in pleasant surroundings. Or should we take seriously the warning: *Woe unto you who add house to house and field to field?* During my childhood, four farms were worked on the land around our house beside the factory; their fields stretched from the outskirts of Eldersli.e. to the foot of the Gleniffer Braes. When I briefly visited there around 1970, some of that farmland was already smothered in streets and houses. The top dam, illustrated on p44 where we once fished and swam, now hopelessly silted up, had almost disappeared. Foul debris – plastic containers, empty cans and other rubbish swirled in the water running over the silt.

I am well aware that some readers may point out that there is no need to weep over the closing of a factory and the building of houses on farmland. They would say that these developments, going on elsewhere in Britain are all for the good.

However, the conflict between rich and powerful city dwellers of Old Testament Jerusalem and the surrounding small landowners, farmers and peasants, is remarkably similar to what is happening to our farmlands today. Edward Hyams seems to agree when he writes (2):

> It so happened that our world, the modern world, was made by the English, a people who used a thorough-going industrial-commercial device to meet the challenge of their condition, and who destroyed their peasantry in carrying the spirit of industry and commerce into their countryside. (Surely Hyams meant *British* rather than *English*).

In controlling the use of land world-wide, power does now indeed seem to be in the hands of the industrialists who are content to see our fertile fields and those who work them disappear, while, in exchange for exports and to the detriment of our balance of payments, we import much of our food. I hope to explore this theme in later chapters. Suffice it to say at the end of this chapter that Christianity began in a garden and that many of our land-use problems may well have arisen because in that first garden the man (and his wife) were tempted to presume that they were smarter than God.

Glenpatrick House in the 1920s

Mary Yellowlees, Tom Mitchell and David Yellowlees
Circa. 1935

David Yellowlees, bridge-building over the Brandy Burn
Circa 1930

REFERENCES

The passages on Stoddard history and on the Gleniffer Distillery are taken from an unpublished brief history of the carpet firm, *Historical Notes on A.F Stoddard Ltd* 1948, compiled by the late J.S.M. Jack, and *The Story of an Unsuccessful Distillery* researched and written by Charles Craig; Ambrosia Books Ltd, 1982.

1. Johnson Paul, *Modern Times,* Weidenfeld and Nicholson 1983.
2. Hyams Edward, *Soil and Civilisation,* John Murray 1976.

CHAPTER 2
GARDEN AND CITY

GARDENER AND ICE CREAM

Soon after our move from Stirling to Glenpatrick, a small stocky man, aged probably in his late forties, came to ask, could he, as gardener in his spare time, keep the lawns, flower beds and vegetable plots which sloped down from the house to the waterfalls. He worked in the factory as a weaver and may have already tended the garden when the house was occupied by the distillery managers. His name was Tom Mitchell; he lived just down the road in one of the staff flats; the garden was to be his life's work and to my brothers and me, he became one of the family. He was a true gentleman and a superlative gardener.

Tom Mitchell was stone deaf, so conversation with him had to be mostly one way. As a child, I suffered from excessive shyness and was a bit tongue tied; maybe I enjoyed his company because as I watched him in the green house, riddling seed mixtures, sowing and pricking out seedlings, there was no need to speak. The family gradually mastered the rudiments of the 'dumb alphabet' and tried to meet the challenge of conversing with our fingers.

Possibly Tom's deafness was partly caused by the environment in the weaving shed where the row of the crashing shuttles was literally deafening. In those days, research had not yet revealed the destructive effect on hearing of long term exposure to loud machinery; ear guards were not worn.

When possible we worked in the garden under Tom's command; we fetched leaf mould from surrounding woodland; we cut the grass, raked, rolled and marked the lines of the blaze tennis court which had been set up by the previous occupants of Glenpatrick House. Friends and relations frequently came for tennis parties.

MOTHER'S ICE CREAM

A feature of these parties was the ice cream made by mother. Ice blocks from a Paisley fishmonger had to be broken up and packed round a central metal cylinder housed in a wooden tub. The ice cream mixture having been fed into the cylinder, wood-bladed paddles for stirring were geared to a handle, the turning of which was quite hard work. I have no record of the ice cream recipe; cream was certainly the main ingredient; it came from a nearby farm where we would call with our milk can and go into the small dairy in the steading where milk had been poured into large wide pans. A metal scoop was used to skim off the surface cream for making butter, and to assist the process, the farmer's wife, Mrs Stevenson, would bend down and vigorously blow the wave of cream to the side of the pan where it was more easily scooped. The taste of the ice cream was delicious.

During World War Two the tennis court became a hen run, carefully tended by my parents

FISHING AND PARADISE

Tom loved trout fishing; he taught us how to cast a fly without disturbing the fish. Some times after heavy rain-fall when the burn was full, he would take us on fishing expeditions "up the burn" which looped and turned through farm land for half a mile or so after cascading down the magical Dusky Glen. To ascend the Glen from pool to pool we had to climb up on the rocks beside waterfalls until we emerged on to the moor top of the Gleniffer Braes from where, on a clear day, one was rewarded by a magnificent view of the Clyde valley framed by the Kilpatrick hills with Ben Lomond and the Grampians beyond. In the 1930s an outstanding feature of the view of the distant Clyde valley could be seen in the huge hull of Cunard's liner, the Queen Mary, being built in John Brown's ship yard. No ships at all are now being built on that part of the river; doesn't this give a cause for *A Time to Weep* over the loss of a Scottish skilled workforce?

There never seemed to be any conflict between duties in the garden and fishing expeditions. Tom was a philosopher; 'What is it,

Watt' he would say 'that makes the fishin' so great'. He would enlarge on the beauty of the burn and the thrill of a rising fish. On Saturday afternoons after work in the garden he and his son-in-law would often stay for a kitchen high tea. On some Sundays, dressed in a suit and wearing a bowler hat he led a kind of ceremonial walk round the garden with his wife, daughter and son-in-law.

To the brothers Yellowlees with their friends and relatives, the Glenpatrick garden, encircled by running water, was a kind of paradise. We swam in the top, largest dam, we fished for trout; we built rafts, coracles, and bridges; we lit endless bonfires and cooked potatoes in red hot wood ash.

I have treasured all my life the glowing memory of those happy family days in the 1920s and early 30s – memories which evidently were not dimmed by travel to distant lands during the Second World War. I had completely forgotten about the copy of a somewhat childish illustrated poem which is reproduced on pages 44 and 45. Someone sent a photo copy of it back to me years ago; it was written in a German barracks in Gluckstadt on the River Elbe, north of Hamburg, where I awaited discharge papers while serving my last months in the army. The original coloured version, sent by me to Tom Mitchell for Christmas 1945 is evidently lost.

THE BEAUTY OF THE EARTH

The low platform of rock below the dam, depicted in the sketch, remains in my memory as a place of an unforgettable experience. I must have been aged 11 or 12 when, crouching there, fishing rod in hand, I first sensed a brief transformation of mood, and kind of exaltation, induced by the sights and sounds around me. Was it the soothing music of the waterfall or the anticipation of the swirl and splash as trout takes the fly? Was it the peace and tranquil beauty of trees, moving water and bird song? Whatever the stimulus, the sensation is hard to describe or to analyse – the sudden flooding of one's whole being with happiness, a feeling of belonging to and being at one with a created world.

I probably did not see my childhood moment of exaltation, as I fished from that rock, as a religious experience; but the awareness of belonging to a transcendent power was very real and when similar flashes of spiritual insight occurred as I grew older, the biblical story of creation took on a new reality. Others who have experienced similar moments will know what the psalmist meant when he sang,

'*Oh Lord, how manifest are thy works, in wisdom hast thou made them all. The earth is full of thy riches'.* (Psalm 104:24)

THE ROAD TO THE CITY

Elderslie stood some ten miles from the centre of Glasgow; travel to the big city through Paisley was easy by tram, train and later by bus and the walk from our home down Glenpatrick road or via a short cut through fields to the Eldersli.e. tram stop took about 25 minutes. Our proximity to a teeming industrial city did not, in those days, bring any threat to our security. From Kilbarchan and Bridge-of Weir in the west, eastward to Paisley and Glasgow, we had many friends living in comfortable houses; I cannot recall one instance of theft or burglary.

In response to critics who will accuse me of fantasising, here is the witness of a GP, Dr. G.R. Robertson who wrote a fascinating book, published in 1970(1) on his experiences in the 1920s and 1930s in a practice including one of Glasgow's well known slum area, the Gorbals:

> '*I never experienced the slightest trepidation in entering any building or house at any time of the day or night, nor have I ever been molested. The Gorbals is rapidly disappearing in favour of handsome new flats, some high, some low. Yet, paradoxically juvenile delinquency has increased sevenfold in the last fifteen years throughout the city of Glasgow and wounds caused by stabbing have multiplied at a similar rate. When I ask old patients who have lived in the district for upwards of forty years what they think of gangs they tell me that in the old days they never gave a thought to going out at any hour of the day or night; they are quick to point out that they would be afraid to do so nowadays'.*

My only experience of inner city practice occurred in 1940 when, as a fourth year medical student, I lived for a few weeks in Edinburgh's Cowgate Dispensary. Under the supervision of the resident doctor students acted as 'general practitioners' for the families living in the teeming slums of the Canongate and Cowgate; in many of the four storey flats, built before the eighteenth century, narrow spiral staircases gave access to unsavoury landings; in some of these the stench of dog and cat excrement was overpowering. But fear of being molested did not exist.

In 1947 I worked as a locum in a practice, serving the needs of a scatter of mining villages on the outskirts of Wakefield, Yorkshire. Again, while doctoring there among the families of miners, I felt perfectly safe.

MINDLESS VIOLENCE

What a contrast to the lives of health workers today. In November 1986 at a special conference called by the Health Secretary to discuss violence against doctors (2) the delegates were left in no doubt that the scale of assaults had reached an all time high. The Health and Safety Department revealed that, during 1985, one in 200 Health Service staff had suffered a major injury requiring medical treatment; five in every 100 had been threatened with a weapon, and one in six were verbally abused.

In 1991 the British Medical Journal published a review (3) of aggression, either verbal or physical, suffered by 1093 GPs in the West Midlands: one quarter of this sample had experienced acts of aggression during a 12 month period. Most of the attacks occurred during home visits at night.

In 1990 Dr. Cormac Swann reported in the journal 'GP'(4) how he had turned out in the middle of the night in answer an emergency call; when he rang the bell of the house where the supposed emergency had occurred a voice from an upstairs window demanded, *'What the bloody hell do you want'?*

When the doctor protested that he had been called out to this house, the answer came, *'No you bloody didn't. No one ill here. Thanks for waking me up. Get lost.'*

Dr Swan's astonishment at what had happened was short lived; when he returned to where his car had been parked, it was not there, but was found undamaged some twelve miles away. It had been used for a carefully planned 'job'. A parked car bearing a *Doctor on Call* notice usually avoids the attention of the police.

These sad trends have happened in spite of vast new housing schemes and a general rise in living standards – infinitely higher than in the 1920s and 30s. Dr. Robertson, quoted above, comments:

> *'The moving about of population from city centre to housing schemes on the periphery and into multi-story flats disrupts the close relationships of many families… the vast majority of people welcome the new amenities, but on the other hand there is more nervous tension than in the old days. Most women are now out working. Children grow up undisciplined and in the belief that life should consist of nothing other than pleasant sensations. When a young women today wishes to have her baby at home she would be hard pressed to find a neighbour willing to come in and sit with her. Indeed she would be lucky if her own mother would be prepared to render assistance, as she would be too busy at her job. How the gods must laugh at us! What they give with one hand they take away with the other'.*

I am not suggesting that in the first half of the 20th century, Scotland was a crime-free Utopia; far from it; but there is no doubt that following the arrival of the "Permissive Society" in the 1960s the increase in crimes of violence and decrease in Christian altruism was real and disastrous.

Political class warriors may see me as a prudish spoilt brat from a white middle class family – (to some writers and broadcasters, "white middle class" has become almost a term of abuse). We three brothers were certainly aware of the unique privilege of being brought up, by loving parents, in such a wonderful place. The contrast of the endless streets of tenements, seen from the top of a tram or bus taking us on occasional trips to Glasgow was heart-rending; here were thousands of families living in an environment totally cut off from the land. Even in my childhood I sometimes experienced a hint of guilt as well as sorrow that so many families were doomed to lives engulfed by soul-less dreary buildings with never the sight of trees, fields or gardens.

City and Rural Desolation

Is not the growth of cities and rural depopulation the greatest challenge facing most industrial nations? Must the benefits of industrial mass-production – bicycles, powered transport, washing machines, central heating and thousands more of essential appliances pouring out from factories, be bought at the expense of the cancer-like growth of cities, ruined farmers and empty farmlands?

As succeeding generations of city dwellers get farther and farther from their roots in the countryside, their intelligentsia and leaders become ever more ignorant of the earth which nourishes them.

Dream of Self-Sufficiency

In the 1970s when monetary inflation, unemployment, and conflicts between management and labour threatened our country with total economic collapse, a small discussion group in Aberfeldy considered what might be done in this valley in the event of such a catastrophe. Could our rural population survive an economic storm? In our upper Tay Valley we had good arable land, freshwater fishing, water power, plenty of hill-grazing for meat, grasslands for milk, mountain or moor for venison, and extensive woodlands.

When the press somehow got wind of this "declaration of independence" a few reporters, eager for a story, descended on Aberfeldy. One of these from a well known daily paper who came to look at a vegetable garden, astonished the gardener by showing great excitement when, evidently for the first time in his life, he saw brussel sprouts actually on a plant; I suppose that he had previously encountered them only on a supermarket shelf. Even more astonishing on a later occasion, was the reaction of an American business manageress to whom I showed my small potato plot; "*Gee*" she said as she stooped to finger the leaves "*and where are the pataters?*" She evidently thought they should be hanging on the stalks!

One reason for weeping over the widening gulf between city and countryside is the difficulty many city people will have in understanding the message of the Old and New Testaments both of which are rich in images of animals, plants and birds. What are they to make of the "Sower who went out to sow", or the lost sheep, or the weeds growing among the corn? And how can young men who have never seen, far less worked on a farm or garden know what is meant by that ringing verdict from Genesis "By the sweat of your brow, you will eat your food." (Genesis, Chap. 3,v 19)

Machines have, thankfully taken some of the sweat out of farming and it would be absurd not to use appropriate technology to ease the burden of physical toil. But is not Edward Hyams correct in his statement, quoted in chapter 1, that *the spirit of industry and commerce* destroyed the peasantry of England? Farmers have every right to respond that if they are to make a living they have to boost output and cut costs and that the "spirit of industry" has made large scale farming in the UK far more "efficient" than the smaller holdings in mainland Europe. As one who has never had to live by farming, I hesitate to pontificate on this subject, but as a doctor, I feel justified in chapter 3 in arguing that aspects of industrial farming will bring "a time to weep."

Poem From Germany -- Walter Yellowlees.

This is the court where we once used to play
In the heat of many
A summers day

And there's the hen house
Built on the court
To provide us with eggs
Instead of with sport

This is the dam where
The Brandy Burn
Pauses awhile as it makes
the turn
Over the fall and under
the trees
Where trout feed on
the fly
In the evening breeze

WAT.

And that's the house
On the Brae as it stands.
Though I've travelled afar
In many Strange Lands
In all of the Countries
Yet have I to see,
A place half as fair
as
Bonnie Glen, P.
~ 11 ~

WAT.

45

REFERENCES

1. Robertson Dr. G.R. *Gorbals Doctor.* Jarrods, London 1940.
2. Feinman J. *News Focus, GP London p18, Nov 1986.*
3. Hobbs F.D.R. V*iolence in General Practice, BMJ, 302, 329-332,1991.*
4. Swan.C, *Danger Lurks in Late Night Calls,* GP May 1990.

CHAPTER 3
LAND USE AND HEALTH

Those who claim that UK farming methods are more "efficient" than on main land Europe, ignore the consequences of industrialised agriculture. If the cost of polluted water, of soil erosion, of ill health in farm animals and humans, resulting from the use of ever increasing quantities of artificial chemical fertilisers and highly toxic pesticides are entered in the balance sheet, claims for efficiency cannot be sustained. How many millions of pounds were expended on the recent BSE and Foot and Mouth tragedies? Would not the slaughter of thousands of cattle have been prevented if organic growing had been the rule rather than the exception?

This is a complex and controversial subject. Why has research, carried out and published in the first half of the 20th century, been ignored? Why is the ground-breaking work of scientists such as Sir Robert McCarrison, Sir Albert Howard, and the American dentist, Weston Price (1), never, ever mentioned in the corridors of power, thronged by those who control our agriculture, medicine, dentistry and veterinary science. The answer to that question must be: the cosy relationship, established during Hitler's war, between chemical firms such as ICI and the then Minister of Agriculture – a relationship which continued after the WW2. (2) No wonder that the virtues of biological farming appear to be strenuously buried in our agricultural colleges.

SIR ALBERT HOWARD

Five years ago I attended a Scottish conference on Organic Farming; in chatting to a member of the staff of the Scottish Agricultural College I mentioned the work of the late Sir Albert Howard and was surprised that this scientist had never heard of Howard. His admission confirmed that the influence which the chemical industry exerts on farming is similar to that which pharmaceutical interests has on medicine – all the emphasis is on the sale of artificial fertilisers to farmers or, in medicine, on the promotion of pharmaceutical products; little attention is given to published research on prevention. I hope that I will be forgiven for repeating, in the following paragraph, what has already appeared in a previous work:.

> *Soil fertility depends on living energies, living relationships in the top few inches of the soil. The most important of these is mycorrhizal association – the fascinating partnership between certain soil fungi and the root hairs of many plants. By penetrating the substance of root hairs these fungi enable the plant to absorb essential nutrients, and according to the work of Howard, to resist disease. Here is one of nature's miraculous living partnerships.*
>
> *Where there is life there must be reverence; the organic grower tries to revere and emulate nature's laws and processes by encouraging mycorrhizal association and by seeking to enhance soil fertility or future generations. This he does by using natural wastes to build up the humus content of the soil and to feed the soil's living population.* (3)

Sir Albert Howard, a distinguished botanist and honorary Fellow of the Imperial College of Science, in 1905 accepted the offer of the post of Economic Botanist at the Agricultural Research Institute, newly founded at Pusa in Bengal, India. He had previously done valuable research at the West Indian Imperial Department of Agriculture where he realised that '*there was a wide chasm between science in the laboratory and practice in the field*'(4) He followed this theme when he observed that the crops grown for centuries by the peasants of Pusa seemed to enjoy remarkable freedom from pests and diseases. So he tried their methods of organic cultivation on the 75 acres of land granted to him by the government; later he wrote: '*By 1910, I had learned how to grow healthy crops, practically free from disease, without the slightest help from mycologists, entomologists, clearing-houses of information, spraying machines, insecticides, fungicides, germicides, and all the other expensive paraphernalia of the modern experimental station*' (5)

The farm animals which Howard reared on his land were seen to rub noses over the fence with neighbouring livestock suffering from Foot and Mouth disease. Howard's beasts remained healthy, thanks, he believed, to the superior fertility of the soil on which their food was grown. Even if critics are correct in suggesting that the

Indian strain of Foot and Mouth virus had far less virulence than that of Europe, the resistance of the organically fed beasts to infection is remarkable.

Not far from here, in Scotland, farmer Ian Miller who converted his mixed farm to organic growing 20 years ago reports that during those years his farm animals have never required the services of a vet (6). Why has it been left to brave volunteers to follow Howard's advice? Why have no Government scientists done farm-scale research on organic growing?

MENACE OF PESTICIDES

The repeated spraying of crops with highly toxic pesticides on industrialised "efficient" farms is not being adequately monitored according to a report, *Pesticides, Chemicals and Health* (1990), issued by the British Medical Association. In a vigorous campaign Georgina Downs has given evidence from many countries, of ill health in people exposed to the drift of pesticide spray. Her lucid lecture to a London conference in 2005 (7) listed the acute symptoms, experienced worldwide, by victims exposed to toxic sprays; they include sore throats, nasal and eye inflammation, skin blisters, headaches, dizziness, nausea and flu-like symptoms. .

Far more serious are the reports, again collected by Georgina Downs, of various forms of cancer, including leukaemia and Non-Hodgkins Lymphoma, occurring in clusters where patients have endured long-term exposure to agricultural sprays. Neurological illness, asthma, and allergies have also been linked to the same cause. It is, of course, difficult to give absolute proof of cause and effect of these illnesses. But surely the evidence is strong enough for adding on to the cost of toxic pesticides a tax hefty enough to guide farmers to the organic alternative.

Since I started writing this chapter, a report of the Royal Commission on Environmental Pollution has been published. Its conclusion, sent to me by Georgina Downs, gives us another cause to weep. The Royal Comission admits that spray drift may be the cause of human illness but instead of advising a complete ban on the use of highly poisonous chemicals, the Commission recommends a five metre buffer zone between the sprayed crops and bystanders. It is well known that air borne spray can travel far farther than five metres; the advice is therefore farcical.

SICK TOMATOES

For years I have grown good crops of tomatoes in the green house in which a heater is essential if the plants, usually reared from my own seed, are to survive in our Highland Perthshire climate. Some 20 years ago I was dismayed to find one morning that the tomato plants suddenly had become unwell. The leaves and top growing points showed gross distortion and shrinkage. Hastily I dug up one of the plants and took it to the office of the Scottish Agricultural College in Perth for a diagnosis. The staff member needed only a glance at my miserable specimen. "Herbicide Spray drift," he said.

I was at a loss to know how this could have happened. Woodland shielded me from the local school on the north and from the main road on the east. On the south, over a farm road, is more woodland, and on the west over a fence and down a steep hill, covered with Elder-berry bushes, is my neighbour's house and garden, with school playing fields and farmland beyond. Enquiries on herbicide spraying at the school, the road maintenance office, and the farm were negative; then I remembered that my neighbour had said something about clearing weeds; when I questioned him he told me that he had used a hand operated pressure spray to shower a bed of weeds with a popular weed-killer. The greenhouse stood at least thirty metres downwind from the sprayed bed of weeds. At the time of the incident my electric *Autoheat Fan Heater* with thermostat control must have blown warm, poison-laden air on to the plants; all of them had to be destroyed.

Tomatoes are known to be very susceptible to herbicide damage; but this "experiment" with weed-killer can apply to pesticides and demonstrates that a five metre buffer zone as safety measure from airbourn poisons is laughable. Do these findings not support the argument for banning altogether the use of deadly poisons in farm or garden?

More Sick Tomatoes

In 1981 the outbreak in Spain of a mysterious illness killed more than 1000 people and left more than 25,000 seriously disabled. The journalist, Bob Woffinden gives a fascinating account of his investigation of this disaster during a visit to Spain in 2001(8). The initial investigation blamed food poisoning, caused by the use of a cheap, imported salad oil. But medical scientists found no evidence of toxicity in the suspect oil and a hospital consultant pointed out in a newspaper article that the symptoms were typical of organo-phosphate pesticide poisoning; he received an immediate telephone call from the health ministry which ordered him to shut up about the cause of the epidemic and to say nothing about organo-phosphate poisoning. There followed a cover up described as *'the prototype fraud that has found echoes around the world' (9)*.

Bob Woffinden reveals how officials who questioned the cooking oil theory were sacked and how the government and chemical industry waged a ruthless campaign of deceit to promote the salad oil theory. In 1983, a commission of enquiry was appointed finally to settle the controversy; to their surprise the commissioners found that in an area where large volumes of the cheap oil had been consumed, not a single case of the illness had occurred. Two of the leading members of the commission were sacked, and the commission ceased to function.

The Spanish cooking oil episode could be taken straight from the pages of Orwell's 1984. For the Spanish government, the news of pesticide laden tomatoes might well have damaged their export trade in fruits and vegetables; the chemical manufacturer's reputation and trade would suffer; the case for organic growing would receive a valuable boost. Officials and traders simply tell lies in order to protect their financial interests. This example of the power exerted by huge multi-national empires over national governments is not unique; the influence of medical scientists, employed by the food industry will be elaborated in chapter 6. "Where is Truth?" is the crux of this matter; how can truth be protected when governments, backed by the food and chemical industry have the money and power to silence those with whom they do not agree.

One truth advocated by Graham Harvey, author of *The Killing of the Countryside*, is the need to encourage the maintenance of soil fertility by supporting mixed farms using traditional rotations and farmyard manure. But evidently three quarters of CAP farm subsidies end up with 10 per cent of the *larger industrialised farms*. (9). No wonder that smaller mixed farms are fast disappearing.

ROBIN'S FARM

Such a mixed farm was Strachurmore, beside the village of Strachur, Argyll, tenanted by my older brother Robin from 1932 until he enlisted in the RAF in 1940. The farm's benevolent landowner, Lady George Campbell, lived in Strachur House standing by the shore of Loch Fyne. Having left school early, then gone to Agricultural College, Robin worked for long spells, on a Scottish sheep farm, on a dairy farm in Denmark, and on the farm of a relative in Canada. From boyhood he had often worked on the farm near Perth of our uncle John Primrose who probably inspired him to be a farmer. During school or university vacations, younger brother Dave and I often went to work at Strachurmore.

The farm comprised about 70 acres of arable land; some 18 Ayreshire milking cows grazed the lower grasslands; as far as I can remember, hay, potatoes, swedes, oats, kale, and other vegetables were harvested. The hill, Cruach nan Capull, in height one thousand eight hundred feet (about 550 m) rising steeply from the river Cur, carried about 900 Cheviot ewes and a small herd of belted Galloway cattle. Pigs and hens were minor additions to the stock.

In the days before the arrival of mains electricity a diesel engine, installed in a barn, generated electricity to drive the milking machine and to give light to house and steading. Brother Dave and I learned how to clean udders and to apply the pulsating suckers to grateful cows whose individual names became familiar. We mucked out the byre, and the stable. Two cart horses and a temperamental tractor gave power for cultivation and carting. We helped to harvest hay and oats, to spread dung, to gather sheep for clipping or dipping and to do the endless odd jobs which are an inevitable feature of farming life. Robin and I found time to enjoy occasional glorious fishing expeditions which involved scrambling along the upper banks of the river Cur; large trout, hovering in deep pools, sometimes rewarded our efforts. Dave preferred keeping down the rabbit populations with his gun.

A full time grieve, Willi.e. McWhirter occupied the bothy and was assisted by a series of 'orramen' and students. Robin did most of the shepherding.

FARM YARD MANURE OR ARTIFICIALS?

At that time, the term, 'Organic,' had not yet come into use; fertility was still maintained by crop rotation and liberal amounts of farmyard manure. In those days many farmers were reluctant to abandon traditional methods and regarded 'artificials' as useful additives but not as replacement for farmyard manures. This stance could claim scientific backing. In 1924 the British Medical Journal had published the findings of Sir Robert McCarrison, a distinguished member of the Indian Colonial Service whose laboratory rat-feeding experiments tested and compared the quality of grains grown on plots fertilised by either farmyard manure or artificial chemicals. After finding that grain grown on the manure plots gave results superior to those receiving artificials, he wrote:

'It is well known to practical farmers and to students of agricultural science that…farmyard manure does something which artificial manures do not and it would seem that this "something" is to increase both the nutritive and the vitamin B value of the grain grown on soil fertilised by it.' (10)

In the light of his findings, McCarrison championed the use of farmyard manure in a memorandum to the Royal Commission on Agriculture in India in which he urged that agricultural research should embrace the health of plants, animal, and humans:

'These are not different subjects but the same subject: a continued story following a natural and ordered sequence from its beginning in the soil, through vegetable and animal life, to its final stage in man, himself.…It is essential that those engaged in agriculture research should be aware of its bearing on public health'. (11)

Was McCarrison's research, done so many years ago, flawed? We may not know the answer to that question, but again, why were not his conclusions tested in the UK by further research assisted by public funds? It was left to the Soil Association, under the leadership of Lady Eve Balfour, valiantly to launch research on a farm scale, which for want of funds, had to be abandoned. (12)

I have no farm financial records but understood that on Strachurmore, profits were meagre. Prices for lambs and wool seemed always disappointing. Robin protested that those who controlled agriculture wanted the country to feed itself by exporting bicycles in exchange for cheap imported food; he was echoing an historian's opinion that:

'The new, industrial-based middle classes of the 19th century held that the proper organisation of human society was one in which Britain devoted herself to the production of manufactured goods, and the rest of mankind supplied her with food and raw material in exchange. The cheaper the latter, the cheaper and therefore the larger quantity of goods sold.' {13}

Industrialists were all for imported food as long as it was cheaper than home grown; cheap food meant lower wages and never mind if farmers went out of business.

BRACKEN CUTTING

Robin, aged 20 in 1934 was not married; the domestic care of the farmhouse was done by a series of housekeepers, friends and relatives; the farmhouse, seldom without staying visitors, vibrated with activity, especially during the summer programme of annual hill bracken cutting, carried out in the hope of reversing the spread of the fern which invaded valuable sheep pastures. Various volunteer bracken-cutters including a group from a Lanarkshire Boys Club came to enjoy this lovely part of Argyll as well as to work on the hill. We will follow them in our next chapter.

Bracken Cutting at Strachurmore Farm.
Nearest figure Robin Yellowlees, top figure Basil Newton,
circa 1940

References

1. Price Weston. *A Nutrition and Physical Degeneration.* Published by the author, Los Angeles 1939.
2. Harvey Graham *The Killing of the Countryside p32* Vintage, London 1997.
3. Yellowlees. W. *A Doctor in the Wilderness p187.* Pioeer Associates(Graphic) Ltd.,Camserney, Aberfeldy 2001.
4. Howard Sir A. *Farming and Gardening in Health and Disease,* Faber, Ltd., London 1944.
5. Ibid.
6. Miller Ian, Jamesfield Farm., Abernethy, Perthshire, 2005 Personal Communic\tion
7. Downs Georgina *Pesticide Exposures.* Green Network Conference, London, 2005.
8. Woofinden Bob. *Cover-up* Guardian Weekend Aug.25th 2001.
9. Charvarial Celine. Oxfam Make Fair Trade *Rich get the Most Subsidies.*
   Dundee Courier. 7th Nov.2005..
10. McCarrison R. *The effect of Manurial Conditions on the Nutritive and Vitamin values of Millet and Wheat Indian J. Med. Res.* 14, 351-78. 1926.
11. McCarrison R. Memorandum on Malnutrition in India…given before the Royal Commission on Agriculture in India 1926. *Report of the Commission vol 1 part 2. 95-119,* 1927.
12. Balfour E.B. *The Living Soil,* Faber 1975.
13. Bryant. A. (1940) *English Saga* p 85, Collins with Eyre & Spottiswood, London.

CHAPTER 4
ROBIN'S FARM, CONTINUED

Edinburgh University was fortunate in its choice of the first Director of Physical Education. The late Colonel R.B. Campbell, an ardent advocate of physical fitness, endeared himself to students who welcomed the opportunity to improve their physical as well as their intellectual skills. We often enjoyed one of the new director's projects, a five p.m. session in a local gymnasium, where students, after sedentary hours in lecture theatres, libraries or laboratories, could for an hour or so, be drilled in strenuous, hilarious exercises and games which concluded with a cup of warm brose.

Ronni.e. Campbell, a distinguished ex-army officer had served in the Boer War and in the Western Front in the 1914-18 war. He found spiritual values in sport and physical exercise; he had excelled as a rugby player, boxer and in fencing; his tremendous enthusiasm, laced with humility and a deep Christian faith gave an inspiring example to undergraduates (1). Since leaving the army, he had made a name for himself as a leader in a Boys Club in London and now, along with his university post he worked with a Lanarkshire Boys Club; he and his hospitable wife kept open house for students at their George Square flat adjacent to the university Student's Union building.

WAR ON BRACKEN

What had he got to do with Robin's Farm? Well, the spread of bracken on the east facing side of the Srachurmore hill greatly reduced the area of grass available to grazing sheep and cattle. In those days, hill sheep farmers hoped that if the young bracken stalks could be cut back annually for at least three years running, the plant would recede – a labour intensive operation. Robin's personality seemed to attract voluntary labour for bracken cutting from friends and relations from far and near. Our mother, a daughter of the reverend Robert Primrose was one of nine siblings, so on that side of the family, cousins abounded. A few of my university friends had come to cut bracken and to enjoy a stay in this lovely part of Argyll.

Colonel Campbell saw in the summer bracken-cutting, a good project for the members of a Lanarkshire Boys Club with which he was associated; they would wage war on bracken and breathe the clean air of hill and glen.

Thus it was that in July 1940 the following entry was written in a very occasional diary which Robin, younger brother Dave and I called "The Strachurmore Chronicles":

July 26th 1940. The gap between this and the last entry is a large one. It cannot be large enough to contain an account of all that has happened. Norway, Denmark, Holland, Belgium, and France have been over run by German armies. At the present moment we await invasion... All this month the farm has hummed with activity; the great bracken-cutting scheme is under way. The yard has resounded with the shouts of many boys and students.

There is no record of the number of Lanarkshire boys who came with their club leader (whose name, I am ashamed to confess, has not been recorded); they and four Edinburgh students slept in the hay loft. One of the four students, the late Dr. Bobby Marquis, in 1944 parachuted into Normandy on D Day as a doctor with the 6th Airborne Division. He landed in an area held by the enemy but managed to regain our lines; post war, he went on to become a distinguished Edinburgh specialist in Paediatric Cardiology. Another student, Basil Newton, had become one of Robin's close friends.

HEADQUARTERS STAFF

For the bracken project, eight people, seven adults and one child, slept in the farm house; they were: Robin, myself, the housekeeper Mrs Campbell, our mother, the Colonel, and two of our cousins, one of whom, named Moira Ekhart, a Primrose cousin, was mother of the child, Martin. Moira's husband had joined the RAF.

Neil Campbell, the colonel's schoolboy son, slept in a tent on the lawn. After war service in Burma he studied at Edinburgh University and then joined the staff of the Brown Trout Research Laboratory, Pitlochry where he made a name for himself as a notable fresh water fishery scientist.

Our mother, whom all loved and revered, in her quiet efficient way, presided over the catering and caring for the bracken army – a daunting task. Luckily the kitchen and adjoining rooms were large enough to take the whole squad at meal times. Without mother's tremendous abilities and help I doubt if the catering would have succeeded. In a previous entry (August 18th 1939) of the "Chronicles" Robin had written of our mother:

Mum is quite extraordinary – no sooner does she arrive here than in one comprehensive glance she takes in whatever most needs doing. Her very presence is gold, myrrh, frankincense and balm of Gilead for a tired soul all rolled into one. There is no one else half like Mum – what other Queen lives, who can so efficiently do the job of a scullery maid, was ever any angel so nearly human or human being so truly angelic. God made man "a little lower than the angels" but the angel was never born yet – if angels are born – or anyway created, who could hold a candle to our mother

By this summer of 1940 brother Dave had joined the Royal Navy; my final year in medicine loomed ahead so clinical experience in Edinburgh hospitals had to take precedence over bracken cutting. On the outbreak of war in 1939, medical students of my vintage were told we must qualify before joining the armed services. During the brief stay at the farm this summer I sensed, even as Hitler's armies were preparing to invade, a wonderful joi.e. de vivre, a sense of purpose as the squad with their cutters or scythes, led by a piper, marched up the road to the hill. The war and the threat to our food supplies from submarine attack may have given fresh impetus to the colonel's scheme. A paradox of war is the sense of purpose and comradeship which can be sadly absent in time of peace.

The war time "Dig for Victory" campaign encouraged farmers and gardeners to expand their growing areas so that our dependence on imported food could be curtailed. (What a pity that it takes a war to promote this policy!).

Unemployment in our cities and idle acres in the countryside have troubled thoughtful people since the start of the industrial revolution and schemes similar to the colonel's have for years been proposed. A film of the bracken cutting, taken that summer, must surely be stored somewhere, but I know not where.

BROTHER ROBIN

Perhaps it was Robin's passion for justice and fair play which ended this brief history; and perhaps he was too impulsive in some of his decisions and yet how I admired his wonderful abilities. His personality, though forceful was always friendly; he championed the cause of farming in Scotland and I am sure would have done great things for farming had he survived. He had inherited his father's love of literature and the ability to memorise and recite favourite poems – mostly Kipling; he could be a forceful and lucid public speaker. He brought a passionate energy to all his doings. Does an unseen hand sometimes provide a relevant document for a struggling writer? As I wrote this chapter I happened to find in an old folder a tattered, faded page dated June 19th, 1936 of Scotland's Sunday Post newspaper. The page carries a report from the Empire Exhibition held that year in Bellahousten Park, Glasgow; it is headed **Australia Beats Scotland in Sheep-Shearing Contest.** A photograph shows two young men on a raised platform, each busily shearing a sheep, while an official in the background holds a stopwatch. (photo on p.)

The report continues: *'Robin Yellowlees, 23 year old farmer, of Strachur, Argyllshire, did his best against Don Munday, champion sheep shearer of Western Australia, at the Wool Pavilion...The contest finished with Don Munday shearing three sheep in 8 min 42.5 sec, against Mr Yellowlees' time of 10 min 42.5 sec He entered the contest because his byre lad had told him about it, and Robin had said –"We can't let these Australians chuck challenges about like this !" He made a great effort, and was loudly applauded by the crowd, which numbered close on 700.'*

Perhaps it was the same kind of patriotic impulse which, in 1940 when the German armies had over-run Europe, compelled Robin to join the RAF. For him the decision must have been agonising. He loved farming and had come to love this part of Scotland and its people; as a farmer his occupation was reserved; he could have stayed. At the end of the Will, dated 24th August 1940, made as he was preparing to leave, Robin wrote.

> "...If I die tomorrow, I die only with the regret that I could not give more to my country than I have done. Those who are left must not mourn me over much for I have ever lived joyously and with an uplifted spirit. I have had the best parents in the world and the best brothers, work which I loved, and health at all times, good friends and an appreciation of all that is and always will be best in this world – what more could a man ask? ... If I am cremated, I want my ashes to be scattered over the hills and fields of Strachurmore"

The following paragraphs are from the final pages of the "Chronicles:"

Monday 29th July. The Colonel held the prize giving for the boys in the dining room after supper. Mum gave away the prizes amid cheers and clapping.

*Tuesday 30th July 1940. The boys departed this morning in procession, piped by me to the road end. No sooner had their backs been turned than mother led a frontal attack on the kitchen... Saturday 3rd August. Robin and Basil returned shortly after dinner on the bike. (*The bike was a motor bike with pillion*) We learned that they had both joined the RAF and were to go to England for further tests on 20th August. Mines were dropped on the Clyde by a German plane on Thursday night.*

Sunday 4th August. There is talk of taking paying guests when Robin goes and the house is empty. The management of the farm will be in Willie McWhirter's hands. Moira is going to stay on and is keen to take paying guests.

September 15th 1940. The boss has been gone about three weeks now and is apparently getting on well in his preliminary training.

By 15th April 1941 in Cowan House, the University Hall of Residence, I was deep in studies leading up to the final exams in June. A letter with ten shillings enclosed came from Ternhill air field, some where in the Midlands, where Robin seemed to be progressing well in his training; he had remembered my 24th birthday. So had Basil Newton who sent a birthday card

On the morning of 20th April our mother, scarcely able to speak through her sobbing told me by phone that Robin had been killed when a training plane in bad weather had crashed into a hill. All the crew died instantly. We heard later that the plane, I think named Myles Master had a bad record. The urgent need for RAF pilots and rushed training may have contributed to the cause of this accident. Some weeks later, Robin's friend, Basil Newton, also died in a crash during training.

On 20th May 1941, my parents and I, with the casket containing Robin's ashes drove by car to Strachur to carry out his last wishes. Brother Dave, on active service with the Navy, could not be with us. Even the time span of over 60 years cannot erase the bitterness and pain of that day. It certainly was A Time to Weep; I wept copiously as I climbed alone with the casket to the top of the hill where so often we had struggled to keep up with Robin on our way to gather sheep; we would talk of all things under the sun and joke and laugh.

After reaching the top and then descending away down to the Succoth burn, I held a remnant of the ashes in the casket. Here was the pool where we paused on our first fishing expedition years ago. I cast the last of the dust into the clear, clear water and watched the white particles as they sank and lay shimmering among the stones on the bottom.

An impulse made me throw off my clothes and dive into the ice-cold water. I swam , came out invigorated, dressed and knelt by the pool to pray; was this a kind of baptism? Somehow my mood of despair and grief, for the moment, was healed.

In the following months another request, written in Robin's Will, was carried out:

"If any stone is to be erected to my memory it shall be a rough piece of rock on the first top of Strachurmore hill going up from the farm. My parents can decide what shall be put on it over and above the inscription: 'For me this land, that sea, these airs, those folk and fields suffice".

For readers unfamiliar with Kipling, the above lines are from The Roman Centurion's Song, AD 300 – an eloquent plea by a centurion whose love for the English countryside and people had grown so strong that he did not at all want to go back to Rome. Here is the first verse.

Legate, I had the news last night – my cohorts ordered home,
By ship to Portus Itius and thence by road to Rome,
I've marched the companies aboard, the arms are stowed below;
Now let an other take my sword. Command me not to go!

My parents arranged for the stone to be placed; they would be deeply grateful for work done to maintain it in recent years by Tom and Cathy Paton, at that time, of Feorline, Strachur. .

A last fitting tribute to Robin comes from a letter dated 23rd April 1941 written to my mother by the late Dr. George McLeod of the Iona Community who had been a guest at Strachurmore. Robin had visited him at Govan, Glasgow and had at Christmas time taken for distribution in the Govan Parish, loads of farm-grown food.

Dear Mrs Yellowlees, So it has happened. Somehow I felt it would, sooner or later, perhaps you did too, perhaps he did. I only know he would never alternatively been happy had he stayed on the farm. No death has moved me so deeply for years as this puritan cavalier. I spotted him to lead young Scotland toward the land again; even at his present age he almost could have done it. He was fierce for justice, scornful of compromise, shocked by pretence; then when it nearly burst him, he laughed…

He has his wings now and I will eat my hat if God allows him to fold them for an hour. Robin's heaven was Scottish earth. God has taken him because even to our dim vision, it was obviously a waste of time to confine him to any local acres of it. Quite simply I believe that he is on new work for Scotland and eternal work. We must not impede his instant progress with it by the one thing that would break his heart – our mourning. This of course is no absurd command that we should be inhuman. Praise be for that gospel that assures us that Jesus wept.

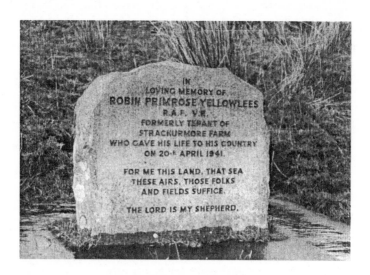

Memorial Stone Inscription

Robin's Memorial Stone, looking south towards Loch Eck

A wild and woolly tussle. ROBIN YELLOWLEES, Strachan (left), and DON MUNDAY, champion of West Australia, in their sheep-shearing contest at the Exhibition yesterday.

Australia Beats Scotland in Sheep-Shearing Contest

The Sunday Post, June 19th 1938

A CHRISTMAS I'LL ALWAYS REMEMBER

IN Iona Abbey there stands a wrought iron candelabra, gifted by his family in memory of Robin Yellowlees, a young RAF officer, who was killed in the Second World War.

Whenever I see it my mind goes back to Govan Old Parish Church on Christmas Eve, 1938.

Earlier that year George MacLeod had resigned his charge in order to found the Iona Community and I was left to look after the work of the parish during the vacancy.

The shadow of unemployment still hung over Govan, as did the far more menacing threat of war.

On Christmas Eve I felt anything but cheerful as I prepared for the usual services.

I had a sore throat and was running a temperature, the ladies who looked after the decoration of the church had failed to appear and one of Glasgow's pea-soup fogs had closed in, shrouding everything in a murky gloom.

Just when my spirits were at their lowest ebb, Robin Yellowlees arrived.

He had driven up through the fog from his sheep farm on the hills above Strachur, his car laden with joints of mutton, white puddings potatoes and vegetables.

He told me that he was haunted by the picture of homes and families in Govan, hit hard by unemployment and the Means Test (the Welfare State and Social Security were still a long way off).

He asked for the names and addresses of some of the people in greatest need and, armed with these, off he went into the fog with his gifts, Father Christmas in a kilt. There was a kind of glow about him.

Tonsilitis notwithstanding, that is one Christmas I shall always remember with gratitude.

It underlined the truth that there is nothing sentimental about the Christmas story.

by
The Very Rev. Dr Hugh O. Douglas

Glasgow Evening
TUE Dec 14

Glasgow Evening Telegraph, Tuesday, December 14th 1976

REFERENCES

1.   *Gray John G.* Prophet in Plimsoles *Edina Press, Edinburgh 1977.*

CHAPTER 5
FARMS GREAT AND SMALL

After my father had made arrangements for the ending of the Strachmore tenancy in 1941, the farm house was used to accommodate American servicemen working on the river Clyde estuary naval bases, and post war, to house the staff of the local hotel. Sheep now graze the arable land where once a variety of crops had been harvested; the dairy cows have, of course, departed long ago; a large area of the hill is planted with alien conifers.

We did not know in those pre-war days that we were living in the twilight of the small mixed family farm. The fate of Strachurmore is shared by similar farms all over the UK – farms which for centuries, gave employment to a huge rural population skilled in caring for the land and its animals. Only a small fraction remain; the rest have gone to swell the populations of ever growing cities; their former homes, steadings and bothies are being converted into comfortable dwellings, some to be occupied by the elderly retired, some for holidays, some for those able, thanks to electronic magic, to conduct their business from a rural setting; the fields which once grew oats, tatties, neeps, and other crops, are merged, especially in the cereal-growing lands to create larger, supposedly more "efficient", prairie farms which use vast quantities of artificial chemical fertilisers, highly toxic pesticides and herbicides.

THE KILLING OF THE COUNTRYSIDE

In his book, *The Killing of the Countryside* Graham Harvey gives a vivid and detailed account of catastrophic rural depopulation. (1) His evidence points clearly to the power wielded by the chemical industry working hand in hand with the UK government. The main objective of these modern-day agri-industrialists seems to be the destruction of the small mixed farm with its traditional crop rotations and natural manures. Subsidies which inflate land prices are lavished on the larger single-crop farms; tax-payer's money helps the purchase of the ever increasing quantities of artificial chemical fertilisers, pesticides and herbicides. Short term increase in yields is bought at the cost of soil erosion, pollution of the environment, destruction of wildlife and the ruin of our soils for future generations. Graham Harvey explains how wealthy businesses buy thousands of acres which are then managed by contract farming companies. As prices per acre increase, substantial profit is reaped from the buying and selling of farm land.

Harvey contrasts the way of the prairie farm with the atmosphere prevailing in some of the few mixed-crop farms, worked by people who are brave enough to defy the artificial chemical regime. Their organic methods survive thanks to support from customers who come from near and far to purchase food which they know is free from toxic residues and which they believe has superior health-giving qualities. These organic growers seem to relish the organic way and have no wish to change. Let us pray that others will follow their example.

North American Vignette

The late Ross Hume Hall, Emeritus Professor of the Department of Biochemistry at McMaster University Canada, was an author, distinguished for his research on human nutrition and for his inspired campaign for dietary/agricultural reform. His lecture, delivered at a meeting of the McCarrison Society in July 1980 at St. Hugh's College Oxford opened as follows:

> "Roy Berry, a farmer near Hamilton Ontario, in 1972 sold his 125 acre farm to a land speculator. The Berry family continued living in the farmhouse situated in the midst of their former farm. The land speculator for the past eight years had leased the farm to York Canners, a large diversified agribusiness. This business farms hundreds of similar leased farms on which it produces vegetables destined for canning. The Berry farm lies on gently rolling land. In Spring, as it dries out from winter snow, the higher portions are ready for working sooner than the lower more soggy parts. When Mr. Berry farmed he watched the weather closely and ploughed and prepared the ground as it became ready. Now, at no particular time in spring, flatbed trucks arrive, discharge equipment and men. Within 2-3 hours the entire farm has been tilled, planted,

fertilised and de-weeded with a herbicide. The equipment and crew disappear not to be seen again until harvest time.

The crop, usually corn, never ripens evenly. Nevertheless, at some instant, day or night in harvest season, trucks laden with heavy equipment roll in and within a short time the entire crop, ready or not, has been harvested.

In this little vignette we note how agri-business regards soil, food and the human consumer. These attitudes play no small part in shaping human welfare because most of the food marketed in western countries is produced either by agri-business or by farmers locked into agri-business methods and marketing schedules. We cannot ignore the attitudes and in this article we explore how they affect the human relation with that from which all life springs – the soil."

Professor Hall's book, *Food for Naught (2)* should be compulsory reading for all medical students and dieticians. In his last paragraph, quoted above, *attitude* is the key word. We could not reasonably object to the attitude of, say, a car manufacturer who uses the machines of mass production to cut labour costs and so cheapen the end product – provided his employees are well treated.

But when our raw material is not inert metal or plastic, but living soil, the industrial attitude will not do. Why not? Because soil fertility depends on nature's law of return – a network of relationships between living micro-organisms, interacting with each other in the endless cycle of birth, death, decay and rebirth to bring forth real fertility. We disobey nature's laws at our peril, as is repeatedly demonstrated in the imbalances, the loss of soil trace elements and other minerals which occur when living soil relationships are disrupted by the use of soluble chemicals. The industrial attitude seeks short term financial gain rather than the maintenance of soil fertility; to quote from Jacks and White: *Men are permitted to dominate nature on precisely the same conditions as trees and plants, namely, on condition that they improve the soil and leave it a little better for their posterity than they found it.* (3)

HISTORY OF RIGHT ATTITUDES

I have referred above to the laws of nature. Human beings were given the intelligence and insights to understand and obey those laws – not always easy; throughout history our ancestors, in dealing with the earth's bounty were, alas, often disobedient. Wisdom often gave way to the attitudes of greed and exploitation, denounced by the prophet Micah (quoted in chapter 1).

Job, probably about 250 BC, was aware of soil erosion:

But as mountain erodes and crumbles and as rock is moved from its place, as water wears away stones and as torrents wash away soil, so you destroy man's hope. (Job.14:18,19.)

The Old Testament author does not suggest that Job's affliction, "Painful boils from the sole of his foot unto his crown" was caused by deforestation and soil erosion, but his possession of "seven thousand sheep, three thousand camels, five hundred yoke of oxen and five hundred donkeys" (Job 1:3) , might not have been very good for the regeneration of plant cover over his uplands and would certainly have led to the erosion which he so vividly describes.

In Job's time, deforestation and soil erosion in Palestine were already a serious problem. Since the days of the Phoenicians, surrounding dynasties had decimated the glorious Cedar forests of Lebanon; they felled and hauled these majestic trees for the building of ships, temples or palaces, but made no attempt to regenerate what they had taken (4).

By early AD, Jewish laws restricted the rearing of sheep and goats in an attempt to prevent over grazing and soil erosion. A Rabbi of those days is on record as teaching: "Those who raise small cattle and cut down good trees will see no blessing". (5)

Jacks and White, quoted above, believed that the fall of the civilisations of Greece, Rome, Mesopotania and others bordering the Mediterranean sea, resulted from the cutting down of hill forests, exhaustion and erosion of soils, and the encroachment of deserts in once fertile lands. It is a pity that these lessons were not learned by our eighteenth century Scottish forebears who felled the forests which once clothed our lovely hill lands and mountains and whose large flocks of goats and sheep prevented regeneration.

So, the lessons of history and of what is happening to our farmlands today, cry out for an organic revolution if we are to rescue our soils from the attitude of the industrialist and our rural lands from desolation. Farmers will protest that "nature's laws" are all very well but, as food producers, they have somehow to make a decent living, especially when faced with the lords of the supermarkets who increase retail profits by refusing to pay for the real cost of production on the farm. They (farmers) might also object to criticism from an elderly GP author who has never himself had to live by farming. By far the largest share of subsidy payments go to prairi.e. farmers, a mere pittance to those with smaller acreages We can only sympathise with those farmers who are forced to "diversify" their activities in order to survive.

As I write today, 16th December 2005, Europe's politicians are trying to conclude yet another summit meeting on the European Union's budget and on the need to reform the European Common Market Policy (CAP). I will not attempt to probe the complexities of the CAP; but must remind readers of its outstanding feature – the fraud and deceit with which it is riddled. At a Probus club meeting years ago in Aberfeldy, the speaker, a senior member of the Scottish judiciary when asked about the truth of a press report which stated that some £6 billion got lost by the CAP through fraud, he replied that the figure quoted was far too small. No wonder that for the last eleven years the EU has failed to audit its accounts.

Commentators have often complained that the CAP favours the small "inefficient" farms of France Germany, or Spain, but a recent press article (Dundee Courier 7th November 2005.) does not support this view.

Here is the press head line: **Rich get the most subsidies, says report.** There follows a statement issued by Celine Charveriat, head of Oxfam's "Make Trade Fair" campaign, quoted in italics:

> ...the Common Agricultural Policy, set up nearly 50 years ago to ensure liveable incomes for Europe's most needy farmers, is handing out hundreds of millions of pounds a year to the most well off. "The CAP is a gravy train for Europe's biggest, richest farmers," said Celine Charveriat... she was calling for a major CAP shake up after new claims that the biggest French farming

businesses swallow up the vast majority of its EU agricultural
subsidies... "This gives the lie to the French argument that it uses
EU subsidies to support its small farmers. They plainly don't"
added Ms Charveriat "Most small French farmers – 70% of them
– get only 17% of the subsidies. "This is as graphic a picture of the
inequality as we've already seen in the UK and Spain."

DÉJA VU

If this report is correct, destruction of small-scale farming does
not appear to be peculiar to the UK. Does not the establishment of
large "Collectives" remind us of what happened in Russia under the
Soviets with such dreadful consequences? The Kremlin dictatorship
saw millions of peasants starve and perish as a result of this insane
policy (6). In the UK the "peasants" did not perish; they simply
faded away into other jobs mostly in the cities. But centralised
control of agriculture from Brussels by an over-paid bureaucratic
elite is uncomfortably like the Soviet model.

DID THEY GO WILLINGLY?

In the 1950s much of our time in the Aberfeldy medical
practice was spent in visiting the scatter of farms in this lovely valley
of the river Tay with its tributary, the river Lyon. Sixty family farms
is a rough estimate of their number in the area served by our medical
practice; some were mostly hill farms rearing sheep and cattle. Some
occupied the flat arable land; about a dozen produced milk for sale. I
doubt if there is now half that number. I have often wondered; did
these farming families happily go elsewhere? Their sons and
daughters evidently have no wish to take up farming as a career.
Would they have stayed willingly on the land if prices at the farm
gate ensured a decent "liveable" income for their exacting toil? Only
those who have farmed here can answer that question; it has
remained unanswered by our politicians.

What is Farming for?

Baffled by the complexities of political arguments over subsidies and the CAP, we, as consumers, should ask a simple question; what is farming for? Here is a simple answer. Farming is for creating and sustaining true soil fertility and for growing as much as possible of fresh, wholesome, unprocessed foods for populations dwelling within national borders. Only when self sufficiency is achieved should surpluses be exported abroad. I hesitate to make this plea as I am not a farmer, but I make it as a doctor who finds himself in "A time to weep" as he joins the queue at the supermarket check-out desk and observes the contents of trolleys. Here is the basic cause of Scotland's sad record of ill-health – endless packets and cans of food and drink which are artificially refined, preserved, coloured, sweetened, and flavoured. No wonder that we lead the world in suffering from diabetes, obesity and clusters of many other degenerative diseases – I doubt if any of the items lifted from the local supermarket shelves come from our local farmlands.

South African Soil Erosion

The dire effects of using industrialised land for growing factory foods occur world-wide. On a memorable visit to South Africa, as my wife and I were being driven through Natal I asked our host, Dr Michael Girdwood, what was the green crop which entirely covered the land as far as could be seen; "sugar cane" he replied.

Later we were taken to a conservation garden, run by a farmer who told us that as a child he would swim and fish in the clear pools of a small river which ran through the garden, downhill from the sugar-cane plantations; but now the pools were so silted that swimming would be out of the question; the sugar-cane fields had, in recent years, been extended by removing grasses, trees and bushes growing along the banks of the river flowing through the fields; thus destroying the check to soil erosion. As we saw from a seaside beach, after torrential rain, vast red stains going far out to sea marked how the foaming rivers carried Natal soil in to the Indian ocean.

We are regularly shown on television, harrowing pictures from sub-Saharan countries of starving families. Am I correct in suggesting that if my answer, given above, to the question " What is farming for?" is correct, in the absence of war or drought, starvation would disappear in sub Sahara Africa as long as priority in land use was given to feeding the people rather than to growing cash crops for export? Am I also correct in stating that certain influential people would reply to my question that farming is above all for sustaining and if possible expanding the output of, the chemical industry?

VEGETABLE PATCH

My vegetable garden here in Scotland, is now limited to four raised beds each about four and a half feet wide and 12 feet long, plus a small green house 6 feet by 10 feet. This tiny patch of soil, in spite of Highland Perthshire's hard winter frosts, grows organically, enough potatoes to feed one adult for about six months, carrots to last about ten months, lettuces from April until November and crops, in season of spring onions, peas, beans, spinach beet, leeks, beetroot, and parsley. The greenhouse gives fresh tomatoes from July until November and enough in the deep freeze with which to make soup during winter. I write this not to boast, but simply to suggest that a source of fresh vegetables exists as an alternative to the supermarket.

References

1. Harvey, Graham The Killing of the Countryside, Vintage, London 1998.
2. Hume Hall, Ross. Food for Naught, Harper & Row, 1974, New York
3. Jacks and White. The Rape of the Earth. Faber, London 1939.
4. Eckholm E.P Losing Ground. W.W Norton, New York. 1976.
5. Hand Book to the Bible. P.15, Lion Publishing, Bearkhamstead. 1976.
6. Tolstoy Nickolai. Stalin's Secret War. Johnathan Cape London 1981

CHAPTER 6
UNFAIR TRADE

Before moving on from farming I feel that readers are due an explanation of recurring phrases in the last chapter and in chapter 3.

NATURE'S LAWS

In the Genesis story of creation, the biblical use of "day" is an undefined measure of time and not the literal 12 hours of 24; thus Genesis is compatible with both the Darwinian theory of evolution and the belief in creation through Divine Intelligence. The drama, acted out in the garden of Eden, is an account of mankind's relationship to the creator God. He has given us stewardship of the earth's bounty with its profusion of plants which Adam "named" – i.e. studied and classified – and gave us ability to dominate all creatures – *'All flocks and herds, and the beasts of the field, the birds of the air and the fish of the sea, and all that swim in the paths of the seas'* (Psalm 8).

Christians who believe in God as the creator of all things must therefore accept that nature's laws are God's laws and that we disobey them at our peril.

Here we come to a question beloved by philosophers. What is nature, and in relation to agriculture and food supply, what can be termed "natural" or "unnatural"? It would surely be ridiculous to suppose that all agricultural use of the land for food is unnatural. If such a belief drove us all to return to hunting and gathering for our food, the human race would not last for long. In any case, when God told Adam that *by the sweat of your brow you will eat your food,* He implied that food for mankind was not there for easy taking, Adam would have to work the land for it. The joke about the Church minister's conversation with one of his congregation is old and oft repeated, but relevant: the minister admires the garden in which Jim is working: "Jim", he exclaims, " the Lord and you have made a great job of this garden", "Aye, minister" replies Jim "and you should have seen it when the Lord had it tae himself." In exploring the laws of God/Nature, in the last 500 years or so, homo sapiens have used to great effect the God-given tools of intelligence, instinct, and curiosity. The invention of scientific instruments – the telescope, microscope, and so on, have revealed to us wonderful things in biology, chemistry, astronomy and physics.

JUSTUS VON LIEBIG

When the German chemist, Liebig, published in 1840 his essay telling how certain soluble chemicals could boost plant growth, the scientific world hailed a breakthrough which had the potential to by-pass the old fashioned notions of conserving fertility by crop rotations and animal dung. Inspired by the German chemist, a young Hertfordshire land owner, John Lawes set up a laboratory in one of his barns, and engaged a professional chemist, Henry Gilbert, to conduct research into Leibeg's theories. The work was soon expanded by the establishment of field plots known as the Rothamsted Agricultural Experimental Station (1). Results demonstrated that the best yields could be achieved by a combination of three chemical compounds of the elements, nitrogen, phosphorus, and potash – NPK, (Kalium is latin for potassium). This conclusion became the accepted wisdom of the farming world.

However, there are aspects of the NPK theory which should have given second thoughts to those who advocated artificial chemical fertilizers in place of traditional "natural" methods of sustaining the integrity of soils. Here are three such aspects.

1. NARROW CHEMISTRY

Liebig, a brilliant chemist, followed the narrow path of chemistry in his exploration of plant growth. In feeding soluble chemicals direct to plant roots, he not only by-passed nature's living systems, he *impaired* one of the most important mechanisms of nature – mycorrhizal association mentioned in chapter 3. Organic growers believe that this impairment explains why chemically grown crops are susceptible to disease as proved by Sir Albert Howard (see chapter 3).

2. Theory and Practice

The Rothamsted experiment is an example of Howard's belief that what happens in a laboratory may not reflect what happens on a farm scale: *'there is a wide chasm between science in the laboratory and practice in the field'*. This truth has been vindicated by the destruction of the integrity of soils, damage to wildlife, wild plants and waterways by industrialised "efficient" farming.

3. The Bias of Commerce

Possibly the most important aspect of The Rothamsted Experiment came in the setting up of the first ever commercial fertilizer factory, established by Lawes; it traded so successfully that it was able to give an endowment of £250,000 to the Rothamsted Experimental Station(2). Here was the start of the sometimes unfortunate link between research in the biological sciences and commerce, a link whereby individual scientists, working in the fields of agriculture, medicine or veterinary science, were often employed by firms whose priority lay in profitable trading and not in the health of plant, animal or human being. Is it not inevitable that a scientist acting for a rich commercial company will be biased in favour of the company's products?

I hope that the reader will not conclude that I am condemning profitable fair trade; my condemnation is directed at those scientists who, for gifts or cash, bend data to please the companies who are trading in chemicals, food or drugs. The link, quickly established between Rothamsted's research plots and profitable sales of artificial fertilizers prevented objective thinking. This subject is so important that, in the following paragraphs, examples are given of how trade often steals priority over truth.

Free Lunches

In 2003 the British Medical Journal featured the close linking of doctors with drug firm representatives, thus: *Free pens and pizza lunches. Sponsored conferences and compromised medical education. Courtesy golf and unaffordable holidays. Thought leaders and ghost writers. These are trappings of doctors and drug companies being entwined in an embrace of avarice and excess, an embrace that distorts medical information and patient care.(3)*

Let us not forget that recent advances in pharmacology, made by drug firm research, have given us a variety of highly effective drugs for treating physical and mental illnesses. But strong evidence in the above quoted issue of the BMJ revealed how the bonding of doctors with well trained drug firm representatives with their free lunches etc. did work in boosting sales. Examples were also given where failure by drug firm reps. to admit side effects of a new drug did, unfortunately – and somewhat tragically – damage patients. I believe that the same "entwining" takes place between scientists, food and chemical manufacturers but much less openly than in the above references. Here are two examples.

MARGARINE NOT BUTTER

In 1977 GPs received an invitation to attend an evening Edinburgh Seminar on "Primary Prevention of Coronary Heart Disease in the Community", starting with sherry at 7.30 pm. There were to be two speakers, a GP and a consultant physician, then a buffet supper. I could not attend, but noted with interest an invitation to a parallel Ladies Programme to be chaired by a Mr. Symington, Flora Brand Manager of Van den Berghs; the two speakers for the ladies were a Mrs Sarah Nolan, Nutritionist, Van den Berghs, and a Mrs Norma Miller, Home Economist, Van den Berghs who would give a cookery demonstration. The event, it seemed, was hosted by Van den Berghs, a multi-national firm dealing in processed oils and margarines. The speaker for the male audience, now deceased, I will name as the late Dr. X, a consultant physician of Edinburgh medical school who did not endear himself to colleagues by appearing to act blatantly as a salesman for Flora margarine. At the time of the seminar he was featured on the TV Scottish News and in the following years, his articles and letters repeatedly appeared in print in various journals including the Scottish Farmers Weekly. His message was always the same – the virtues of polyunsaturated margarine and the terrible dangers of consuming dairy produce – it was a crime, he wrote, to give whole milk to school children. One of his assertions in the Scottish Farmer about heart disease and sugar consumption in the Carribean islands was untrue.

Dr. X had signed himself as "Research Fellow in Preventive Cardiology" of Edinburgh University. When I contacted the office of the Dean of the Faculty of Medicine to ask for the address of the Department of Preventive Cardiology I was told that no such department actually existed. "Then who is paying Dr. X?" I asked. I was advised to ask that question to Dr. X. When some time later I did ask him, he replied that he was "paid by the Department." I later learned from a secure source that cash had been the motivation for his margarine campaign.

CHEMICALS AND CANCER

This second example is again from a professor of (alas!) Edinburgh University, namely Anthony Trewavas of the University's Institute of Cell and Molecular Biology. In 2001 in a lecture to a meeting of the Scottish Group of the McCarrison Society he repeated an incredible statement; it had a few days previously been published in the Daily Telegraph: *'Cancer rates have dropped 15% during the era of synthetic pesticide use.'* When asked by a member of the audience if his "15%" drop referred to cancer incidence, i.e. the number of cancers registered, or to mortality rates, the number of deaths, he seemed a bit confused and muttered something about mortality rates being the only thing that mattered. Whatever he actually meant his statement can best be termed a monstrous lie. In 1999 the British Journal of Cancer, reviewing cancer trends since 1970 stated: *'Incidence rates have increased at all ages in each sex...In children, incidence rates have increased by about a third'.* The Cancer Registration Statistics of Scotland 1986-1995 stated that now approximately one in three people develop some form of cancer. Thus cancer of all organs except the stomach is known to have greatly increased in recent decades. The professor's false statement in 2001 is all the more remarkable in the light of what happened in 2000 in the Queen's Bench Division in the High Court of Justice when Lord Melchett and and Greenpeace Ltd. successfully sued the Glasgow Herald for publishing Professor Trewavas's falsehoods.

Here is the statement for publication in all editions of the Herald, following the reading of the statement in Open Court:

> 'On 3 November 2000 the Herald published a letter it had received from Anthony Trewavas, Professor in Plant Biochemistry at the University of Edinburgh. The letter alleged that Greenpeace campaigns had deliberately spread unfounded fears about GM Foods, so as to further the financial interests of Lord Melchett and Greenpeace, that Greenpeace accepted donations from companies and had inappropriate links with commercial organisations. The Herald acknowledges that there is no foundation in any of these allegations. The Herald recognises that the letter should not have been published and offers its apologies to Greenpeace and Lord Melchett for its publication. Lord Melchett had agreed to donate his damages to charity; the Herald has also agreed to pay the Claimant's legal costs.'

After this legal rebuff, one would have thought that the professor might have refrained for a while from his campaign for artificial chemicals. But here is a headline in the Dundee Courier for 27th September 2002, *Scientists Deride Organic Claims*; a report followed on the first ever conference organised in Scotland by LEAF, standing for "Linking Environment And Farming." Letters by LEAF enthusiasts had already appeared in the local press; their content looked suspiciously like an attempt to destroy the case for organic farming; a farmer friend obtained for me a specimen of the LEAF brochure; sure enough this glossy pamphlet bore on the cover page the word "Bayer", a well known German pharmaceutical company which apparently backs the campaign against organic farming.

I do not know if professor Trewavas receives payment for his campaign in favour of "artificials". He was, of course, the main speaker at the LEAF conference. He told the audience that since the 1950s when chemical farming became widespread "life expectancy had increased significantly". He did not add that since the 1950s, in the UK, we have suffered a catastrophic increase in coronary heart disease, diabetes, asthma, eczema, and above all, cancer. There is no absolute proof that chemicals used as fertilizers or pesticides have caused these diseases. But for cancer, the research by McCarrison in India demonstrated that in a population whose isolation forced them to use only organic methods for their food supply not a single case of abdominal cancer occurred in the seven years he acted as their doctor(4). In 1960 Stefansson published a similar account of cancer freedom in an isolated population in the Canadian Arctic (5)...

PEASANTS

If any farmer ever reads what I have written and agrees with my theme, he or she might object to an organic grower being identified in chapter 3 with the peasants, mentioned by Sir Albert Howard. By the traditional use of composts the "peasants", studied by Howard, had for centuries harvested disease-free crops. The Chambers Dictionary defines a peasant as "a small farmer, a tiller of the soil, a countryman, a rustic". This certainly fits the family farmers who, until the 1950s and 60s worked and lived here in Perthshire. The further definition "a low-born or low fellow" does not apply to the "small farmers" whom I knew and respected; they were far more high-born than some of the characters who today dominate our media; and note the long list of distinguished scientists and writers who were reared in small rural communities – Sir James McKenzie, reared in a Perthshire farmhouse, who rose to be one of London's top cardiologists, Sir John Fraser from a small north of Scotland village, who became head of the department of Surgery, Edinburgh University, Dr. E B Jamieson, author, from Shetland, of world-famous books on anatomy, Alexander Fleming, discoverer of penicillin; he was seventh of the eight children fathered by an Ayrshire sheep farmer. Many more could be added to this list. The small farmers have gone because, as already stated in previous chapters, an economy under the control of city based industrialists demands cheap food which is wrongly seen as a product no different from any other imported thing. In the UK only 63% of our food is home grown; to meet the demand for organic food a considerable portion of such food has to be imported. The activity of Professor Trewavas, described above can, in my opinion, only be explained as part of the response of the chemical industry to the threat of a growing demand by consumers for organically grown food.

The most disturbing thought at the end of this chapter is pity for the ordinary shopper who may want to do her or his best for the family. What are they to make of the often conflicting advice coming from high ranking university academics; and what do they know of the motives of these scientists. Where is truth? *Where shall wisdom be found?*

REFERENCES

1. Balfour, Lady Eve. *The Living Soil.* Faber & Faber, p 134, 1975
2. Jenks, J. *The stuff Man's Made of,* Faber & Faber p59 1959.
3. BMJ *Editorial, No more free lunches.* Vol. 326. p1155, 2003.
4. McCarrison R. *Faulty Food in relation to gastro-intestinal disorder:* Sixth Mellon Lecture, University of Pitsburgh School of Medicine. Nov. 1921.
5. Stefansson V. *Cancer: Disease of Civilisation.* Hill and Wang New York 1960.

CHAPTER 7
FALSE PROPHETS

*Watch out for false prophets. They come to you in sheep's
clothing, but inwardly they are ferocious wolves.*

(Matthew 7:15)

RICHARD DAWKINS

In devoting the last three chapters to farming and to the conflict
between chemical and organic systems, I may be accused of straying
rather far from the main theme set out in my introduction – the
decline of Christian faith in our country during the second half of
the 20th century. As I inwardly debated how best I should return to
religion, it seemed as if an unseen hand had guided me to glance at
the day's television offerings (9th Jan 2006) and to point a finger at
Channel 4's programme, "The Root of all Evil". So I sat and
watched this harsh and bitter criticism of Christianity and all other
religions by the well known atheist, Professor Richard Dawkins. To
him *religion* is the root of all evil.

I do not remember the name of the author who said "Those
who deny the existence of God, do not believe in nothing – they will
believe in *anything.*" In other words, human beings are so created
that they cannot help seeking something to worship; the need for
religion is built into the hearts and minds of atheists as well as
believers.

PRIMITIVE GODS

Do archaeologists ever fail to find religious artefacts in the
settled populations of pre-history? Earliest written records confirm
the universal search for gods. In the days of ancient Greece and
Rome a whole crowd of gods were worshipped in groves and grottos.

*With gods in every grove and fountain, and on every mountain
summit, with gods breathing in the winds and flashing in the lightning,
or in the ray of sun and star, heaving in the earthquake or November
storm in the Aegean* (1) ...

The worship of Mithras, the Persian sun god, rivalled the early Christian church in the opening decades of AD. People in those far off times, utterly dependent on their own crops for food, looked to and worshipped the sun for warmth and survival. Friends who once farmed deep in Glenlyon lost the sun behind high mountain tops from around early November until the glad day in February on which they held a party to welcome the return above mountain ridges of bright rays of sunlight. Today's farmers in highland glens can understand why the Bronze Age people who lived in highland Perthshire some 3,000 to 4,000 years ago, set the standing stone circle, a few miles from Aberfeldy to the movements of the sun, as did the people of Stonehenge.

Much of the Old Testament account is based on historical events; Sir Charles Wolley's amazing excavations in Mesopotamia has confirmed that the flood of Noah's time was no fairy tale; its footprints were uncovered deep under ground in a thick layer of clay. Sound archaeological evidence also confirms the Biblical account of the total conquest by 585 BC of the land of Judah. Excavations of the site of Babylon (in modern Iraq) yielded clay tablets confirming in writing the biblical account of the rebellion against Nebuchadnezzar, king of Babylon, by Judah's king, Jehoiakim.

The Babylonian army destroyed Jerusalem, plundered the temple and all but a few of the inhabitants of Judea were deported to Babylon.

The author of *The Bible as History*, Werner Keller, ends the account of conquest of the holy land and the deportation of its people to Babylon thus: *the story of the children of Israel is at an end – the story of the Jews begins* (2)

BABYLON YEARS

As captives, the Jews soon displayed their devotion to God, their abilities for survival, and their genius for commerce. They were without a kingdom, but were well treated in Babylon and were told by the prophet Jeremia: *This is what the Lord almighty, the god of Israel, says to all those I carried into exile from Jerusalem: Build houses and settle down; plant gardens and eat what they produce...seek the peace and prosperity of the city to which I have carried you into exile* (Jer. 29; 1-5) Their success in obeying these instructions is recorded on ceramic tiles bearing written records of lists of goods, of accounts, conveyancing, loans, businesses, and of names of Jewish firms (3). They certainly sought prosperity and when king Cyrus took over the Babylonian empire, he rewarded the Jews by assisting their return to Judea in 537 BC. Were some of them even reluctant to leave their Babylonian houses and gardens?

The advice to plant gardens made sense at a time when Babylon, standing near the river Euphrates was still part of *the "Fertile Crescent" – the centre of civilisation from the Stone Age right up to the Golden Age of Graeco-Roman culture.*(4) Rich fields of corn and barley, market gardens, date palms and fig trees abounded, all irrigated by a complex network of channels and ditches bringing water from the two rivers, Tigris and Euphrates. The land around cities built near the two rivers was green and fertile 500 years before the coming of Christ. Irrigation channels had been there since the Neolithic age. Today, these lands are howling deserts of sand dotted with mysterious mounds which in modern times were eagerly excavated by archaeologists from France, Britain, Germany and the USA. Their skills were rewarded by the appearance, after careful removal of rubble, of extensive walls, foundations of towers, streets, houses, palaces, idols and fountains of once fabulous cities – Babylon, Ur, Nineveh, Mari and others.

Why, when and how was this land of plenty turned to desert? According to Erik P. Eckholm of the World Watch Institute (5), crops failed because of neglect of the irrigation systems. Ditches and channels were not cleared of silt; water movement slowed and allowed salt deposits to accumulate on soil surfaces; the land became a sterile desert.

The above quotations from Keller's *The Bible as History* are included in this chapter in the hope of persuading atheists such as Richard Dawkins that the bible is not all about "Myths". The biblical account of the struggles, wars, conquests and defeats endured by the tiny kingdom of Judah at the time of theBabylonian captivity is convincingly proved by modern archaeology to be correct. Thanks to archaeology the biblical account of names and places is true history.

CAESAREA PHILLIPI

The climax of that history came with the birth of Jesus whose claim to be the Son of God, could only have been made either by someone mentally deranged, or by the unique, one and only human being who embodied God's ultimate truth and purpose – the light of the world who "dwelt among us". The confirmation of the claim of Jesus is told in Matthew's gospel (Ch.16:13-17) when, in reply to His question "Whom say ye that I am" Peter, the fisherman, answered "You are the Christ, the son of the living god".

The place chosen by Jesus to put His question is of great significance. Caesarea Phillipi, was famed at that time as a centre for the worship of the god of nature. Its towering hills, mysterious caverns, and deep springs, said to be the source of the river Jordan, gave a backdrop of awe and wonder. Here the Caananites had worshipped Baal and called the place Balinas; later, the Greeks identified it as the birthplace of their god, Pan and named it Panias. (6) By New Testament times the Romans had built a huge temple there, to the glory of Caesar, so Herod's son, Philip, changed the name from Panias to Caesarea Phillipi. This was the place, in the shadow of a temple for worship of a human emperor and surrounded by the shrines of the Pagan Gods of Nature, where Jesus made the declaration of his identity as God's Son who became flesh and dwelt among us. From now on, he explained to the astonishment and dismay of his disciples that "...he must go to Jerusalem and suffer many things at the hands of elders, chief priests and teachers of the law, and that he must be killed and on the third day raised to life." (Matt.Ch 16:21)

The Roman Empire did not last; the gods Pan and Mithras with all the other gods beloved by Greece and Rome remain only in the mouldering ruins of temples and crumbling sculptures; against all the rules of earthly probability, the young Rabbi, the carpenter of Nazareth with his small band of humble followers who fled in panic at the hour of his arrest, was to found a spiritual kingdom whose bounds know no end.

We are told by Luke (Acts 1: 15) that after the ascension of Jesus when Peter took over the leadership of the small band of his followers they numbered one hundred and twenty.

DECLINE IN THE WEST

It would have seemed beyond belief to that tiny group that in two thousand years, world-wide, the estimated number of Christian followers of all denominations would have reached 2.1 *billion.* In parts of Africa, Asia, South America and China the Christian faith is spreading. In 'developed' Europe, including Britain, however, the decline in our Christian believers during the second half of the twentieth century is as dramatic as the increase elsewhere. We are not less religious than we were; humanity, I repeat, is bound to worship something and as we Europeans abandon the truth of God's presence and providence, other false gods take His place. The list of these false gods is almost as long as that of the pagan gods of Greece and Rome.

Richard Dawkins' performance on TV is an example of a false prophet in action. He worships *Science Linked to Atheism;* these deities lift him far above any thought of the creator God; he sees himself to be intellectually far too grand to stoop to belief in a spiritual world. Of course, it is right that the extraordinary benefits to humanity achieved by scientists in the last three hundred years, are to be admired; but Dawkins blatantly breaks the simplest rule of science which forbids scientists to select and distort evidence in order that their own preconceived ideas should prevail. He makes no attempt to balance his intense hatred of Christianity by praising achievements of the Christian religion, such as education, medical care, family stability, law and order, freedom of speech, abolition of slavery not to mention the quiet, unsung devotion and work of countless Christian congregations of all denominations here and abroad. No, Dawkins has no wish to *act justly love mercy and walk humbly (7)* but devotes much time in his programme to scenes of two events, obviously selected to persuade viewers that Christianity is ridiculous.

Two Events

The first event takes place at Lourdes in southwest France where annually thousands of sufferers gather in the hope of healing from the spring water issuing from the Grotto of Bernadette. The second, from USA, is a meeting of a large, noisy congregation revelling in an extreme form of American evangelism.

Both events are interesting but have little to do with "main stream" Christianity. It may be uncertain whether or not real miracles happened at Lourdes; the account of the vision, told in the book "The Song of Bernadette," is charming and well worth preserving.

As for the American congregation led by a rather dour looking speaker whose name I did not record, the atmosphere, for me, was too close for comfort to the mass hysteria and ecstasy usually associated with various strange cults.

Grim Experiments

Why, as a scientist, did Dawkins make no reference to the large scale socio/economic "experiment", started in Russia in 1917, when a government of political scientists and atheists seized power. They did their best to abolish the Christian faith in that country by persecuting believers, destroying church buildings or turning them into museums. Many starry-eyed intellectuals and atheists hailed the Russian experiment as the dawn of a new age of enlightenment. Some of them came back from visits to Soviet Russia, where they were shown carefully selected projects, with glowing accounts of this wonderful regime.

As became clear in later decades, Communist Russia represented one of the most hellish regimes in all history, the numbers slaughtered at the whim of Lenin, Stalin and others are estimated in millions (8).

Soviet Schools and Hospitals

When, in 1999, Melita Norwood was exposed as a Soviet spy working in Britain, she declared "I did what I did ...to help prevent the defeat of a system which had given ordinary people education and a health service." In 1988, after 70 years of Communism/atheism, *Pravda* reported: "21% of our schools are taught in premises without running water, 40% in premises without sewage facilities. Some schools operate a shift system, as there are too many pupils for the facilities available."

In the same year, 1988, the Soviet Health Minister announced: "In more than half the country's medical establishments there is no hot water or mains drainage. Citizens frequently complain angrily about the poor quality of the doctors, the need to give bribes, and the filthy conditions in the hospitals." (9)

The second, similar experiment came in the 1930s when Hitler seized power in Germany and soon plunged Europe and then Asia into the Second World War.

Both of these regimes sought to replace Christianity by what may be termed "Caesar Worship" – dictatorships which elevate the leader to the status of a god; Christian believers are persecuted, churches closed, and pastors locked up or executed. At regular gatherings of Caesar-worshipers such as at Nazi Nürnberg rallies, the throng of believers, by flags, music and marching, are whipped up into a frenzy as their leader god appears to address them.

The Permissive Society

Nearer home, in the 1960s, a British phenomenon, akin to a social experiment, profoundly altered our national life. Richard Dawkins has not, evidently, studied the arrival of the "Permissive Society" powered by a philosophy hostile to the Christian faith. No political party launched this experiment; but neither church nor state seemed willing or able to halt it. The events and philosophies, listed below, contributed, in my opinion, to the terrible moral decline of the second half of the 20th century.

1   The *Humanist Manifesto* of 1933, (repeated in 1973) provokes, not A Time to Weep, but a time to be appalled and justifiably angry. The hidden agenda of the Humanists is: *permeating the teaching of schools in Britain and elsewhere in the world: ....its aims are to organise a totally secular "religion" without any Christian or moral teaching on a worldwide scale....People must have the absolute right to suicide, abortion, divorce, euthanasia, and sexual freedom....any varieties of sexual behaviour, both normal and deviant should be explored and should not in themselves be considered evil. The aim is for children to absorb such sexual information as early as possible. This should be done through the influence of specially trained teachers, **without any reference to Christian and moral principles that parents might desire for their children.** (Emphasis mine, WY)

> The Humanist Magazine Jan/Feb 1983 stated ....*The battles for humanity must be waged and won in the school class room by teachers who correctly perceive their role as* **the proselytisers of a new faith...** *the classroom must and will become an arena of conflict between the old and the new....the rotting corpse of Christianity...**and the new faith of Humanism** (10)

2   In 1966 David Steele's (now Lord Steele) Amendment of the law on abortion brought about abortion on demand. The total number of foetuses destroyed in the womb now totals more than 5 million. No wonder Scotland's population is falling.

3   In 1962 the Reith Lecturer, a distinguished psychiatrist, on the theme of *This Island Now,* told the nation that sexual intercourse before marriage was to be recommended to young people. (11)

4   From the late 1950s, television receivers were being installed everywhere, giving "false prophets" a new medium for undermining Christian values.

5   Huge tower blocks arose around our cities. Their dire effects on family life, seen by a GP, are recorded in chapter 2 above.

How widespread is the "Hidden Agenda" of the Humanists? Events 2, 3 and 4, above seem to be echoing the tune of the Humanist song sheet.

Identifying Humanist school teachers as "wolves" is no exaggeration; those false prophets of the permissive society urge children to rebel against their Christian parents and do what they want with their lives, uncaring of all authority except Humanism. They are bringing to school children a "new faith"; their language confirms the view that the human need for a religious "faith" of some kind, however anti-Christian, cannot be avoided. Other events of the 1960s Permissive revolution can probably be added to my list, but how strange that Dawkins did not touch on consequences of the atheist revolution which sought to abolish all Christian teaching.

REFERENCES

1. Manuscript on ancient Greece; source unknown.
2. Keller W. *The Bible as History p285* Hodder & Stoughton 1967.
3. Ibid p287.
4. Ibid p27.
5. Eckholm Eric, *Losing Ground W Norton & Co,Inc New York 1976.*
6. Barclay W. The Daily Study Bible, Matthew 2. p135
7. Micah. Ch 6:8..
8. Nielson N.C *Solhzenitzen's Religion.* A.R Mowbrey, Oxford 1976.
9. Harvey J. *A Wasted Life.* Daily Tel. Letters, 15/09/99.
10. *The SIECUS CIRCLE.* Belmont, Massachusetts. 1977.
11. Carstairs M. *This Island Now* Hogarth Press, London 1962.
12. *SIECUS* stands for Sex Information and Education Council of the US
13. A Humanist Revolution – Destruction of Life, Family and Society.

CHAPTER 8
BY THEIR FRUITS

In warning us against false prophets, – the wolves in sheep's clothing – Jesus added "by their fruits you shall recognise them. Do people pick grapes from thorn bushes or figs from thistles?" Barclay reminds us (1) that the flowers which top certain thistles do indeed look like figs, and that the small black berries of the buckthorn bush might well be mistaken for miniature grapes, but for food, both are bitter and useless; in the same way, the message of false prophets may at first appear attractive, but in the end, comes bitter disappointment and disaster. Here are some of the bitter fruits, harvested from the atheistic teaching of permissive society prophets.

CRIME

The graph on p20 confirms the disastrous moral decline which began in the 1960s. It shows official figures of "Crimes and Offences" made known in the UK between 1940 and 1994. There was little change in numbers in the 1940s and 50s then came the sudden and dramatic rise in the 60s. An increase of this magnitude is surely real and not due better detection. The dreadful increase in the drunken and sometimes drug induced violence in the young of both sexes no doubt contributes to the high levels of crime.

STD

The permissive prophets are aided and abetted by the sex education industry the main activity of which seems to be the sale or free issue of condoms; and, of course, the provision of the contraceptive pill to younger and younger girls. Never, oh never even a whisper of the wisdom of chastity before marriage. The prophets evidently have learned nothing from Sweden where compulsory sex education for children over 10 years old was launched in the 1950s. The years following this initiative saw a significant increase in the incidence in Sweden of syphilis and gonorrhoea especially among teenagers aged from 15 to 19, also an increase in illegitimate births and requests for abortion. (2)

The same thing has happened in Britain. Sexually transmitted disease, STD, which we used to call Venereal disease, ("VD" to medical students), is more prevalent than ever. In 1972 a specialist on the subject reported record numbers of cases coming to his clinic. The reason for this disastrous increase in serious disease, in his opinion, was the growing, casual attitude to sexual intercourse; it was often impossible to trace the infected contact from whom a patient had acquired the disease because the patient did not know the infected person's name and address, nor anything about him or her. (3)

The late professor Ian Donald, of the Chair of Midwifery, Glasgow University, whose text book on the management of child birth, is a masterpiece of clarity, confirms the sad results of permissiveness. In a Daily Telegraph feature article (1978), he gives an account of some of the consequences associated with the introduction of the contraceptive pill – unprecedented numbers of abortions, of illegitimate births and of sex crimes. He writes: *Perhaps the most disturbing feature of all this is that it is the youngest teenage groups who are suffering most, not only numerically but in terms of venereal disease, pelvic ill-health, attempted suicide, disillusionment and misery, predominantly female.(4)*

APHRODITE AND VENUS

Would Richard Dawkins, the scientist, with his band of atheists/humanists agree that when Christian values are cast aside the results are terrible; would they also agree that in the UK, having abandoned the God of the bible, many of our people including media pundits are turning to a popular goddess of the ancient world, Aphrodite in the Greek language, Venus in Latin? When Paul journeyed to Corinth he faced the daunting task of bringing Christianity to a city, famous for debauchery, sexual licence and drunkenness. "*Dominating Corinth, stood the hill of the Acropolis. The hill was not only a fortress; it was a temple of Aphrodite. In its great days the temple had one thousand priestesses of Aphrodite who were sacred prostitutes and who, at evening, came down to the city streets to ply their trade. It had become a proverb, 'No man can afford a journey to Corinth."* (5)

As in the ancient world, today's exploiters of Venus are driven by the promise of financial gain from the trade in sex. They are encouraged by vendors of contraceptive pills and condoms whose business flourishes under the banner of "Sex Education".

I must here suggest that as for Venus and Aphrodite almost all the idols featured below are closely entwined with a super deity – the god of cash and worldly wealth.

MAMMON OR WORLDLY WEALTH

When Job wondered out loud with such anguish, why God had punished him so sorely, although innocent of wrong doing, he gives a very long catalogue of sins, for which he would have deserved punishment; one such sin was worship of worldly wealth: *"If I had put my trust in gold or said to pure gold, 'You are my security' If I have rejoiced over my great wealth, the fortune my hands had gained."* (Job .31: 24,25) He admits that he is wealthy but protests that he does not "rejoice" over the fact; he tells that his wealth enables him to pay good wages to his staff and that he has not made a supreme idol of his "pure gold". His attitude to his riches confirms that *Job was blameless and upright; he feared God and shunned evil* (verse1). Making wealth by honest means is surely not a sin, it is the *attitude* to wealth that matters.

In his *Epistle to a Young Friend,* Burns echoed Job's thoughts on wealth when he advised his young friend to make money:

> *Not for to hide it in a hedge,*
> *Nor for a train attendant*
> *But for the glorious privilege,*
> *Of being independent.*

The "glorious privilege" of Robert Burns surely includes the privilege of being able to give to good causes and so to obey the words of Jesus that it is better to give than to receive. But today there is a problem for givers to charity; I hesitate to venture into political/economic realms by agreeing with economists who teach that giving to good causes would raise far more cash if the State did not tax everyone so heavily.

WHY NATIONS DECLINE

A statement by the late Sir J.B.Glubb, soldier, diplomat, and author, which I have quoted in a previous publication, (6) bears repetition here. Glubb wrote, on the decline of nations:

> *Long periods of wealth and power corrupted these nations; money became more important to them, replacing the old standards of honour. Their wealthy descendants, living in luxury, saw less need for Divine aid. Religion became a sheer formality, sexual morality was abandoned and money assumed paramount importance. Crimes of violence became everyday events. The leaders ceased to be statesmen and became politicians, bribing, lying, and intriguing in pursuit of their private interests. The exact repetition of signs of decline are amazing... .for example, the public infatuation for athletes, actors, and singers which is recorded of the Greek empire, Rome, Byzantium and the Bagdad of the Kaliphs.*

I implore readers to note that my false prophets with their false gods, include some activities which are admirable; the fault is not in the activity but in its elevation to the status of a deity to be worshipped to the exclusion of Christian truths. Infatuation for, "athletes, actors, and singers" as described by Glubb, might be added to my list of modern idols; Caesar worship with attached Fascism and Communism, sexual licence, Humanism, and the worship of money have been briefly discussed as "religions" which replace Christianity; to them could be added: the Occult, Astrology, New Age worshipers, animal rights activists, drug worshipers, Freud's psychoanalysis.

(Oh! For a W.S.Gilbert who could compile a new "little list" of people who "never would be missed!")

ATHLETES

I hesitate to include athletes or sportsmen and women among pagan idols but, as in the case of wealth creation, it is not the sport per se which is at fault but the infatuation verging on worship. Athletics and team sports are God-given gifts; a dreadful fault of state education lies in its failure to give pupils adequate training and encouragement in athletics and sport. But, in the last fifty years, has our sport been so corrupted by money and media attention that a serious decline has occurred in standards of decency and what we used to call "sportsmanship".

James Bartholomew has given a well researched account of the decline in the behaviour of professional footballers in the last 50 years. Violence and cheating had become so prevalent by 1982 that the authorities tried without avail to stem the tide.

Bartholomew gives sound evidence that from 1891/2 up to 1961/2, in league football "sendings off" by the referee averaged about 12 per annum. But in the early 1960s things began to get much worse – here we are again at the 1960s start of the permissive society! – by 1979/80 sendings off numbered 115; in 1990/91 they had risen to 200. In the latest year for which figures a available the count is 451! It must be A Time to Weep when a footballer who repeatedly cheats and behaves on and off the field as a violent thug is treated by the media, not as a miscreant, but as a hero. (7)

Am I too sensitive and soft hearted to want to weep when professional cricketers and their admirers see no wrong in encouraging fielders to "sledge", i.e. to shower verbal abuse at their opponent's batsman in order to spoil his concentration, or see no wrong in encouraging their fast bowlers to aim their bouncers at the batsman's head or chest. (Yes, I know that it was England's Test team, captained by Jardine who launched "body-line" bowling many years ago against Australia's Don Bradman). Comment on "Infatuation for Actors and Singers" must be left to readers' better qualified than this author. Is it a defect in my appreciation of music to feel A Time to Weep as I hastily switch off the TV at the appearance of some (drug-crazed?) Pop star idol. Another threat to Christianity, perhaps the greatest of all is the rise of Islam in Britain in recent decades, to be discussed later. In the meantime Freud deserves mention.

FREUDIAN THEORY

Sigmund Freud, (1856—1939) the famous Austrian physician and neurologist cast new light on the workings of the human mind. His theories, expounded with great skill and clarity, profoundly altered our vision of how our minds work and postulated the enormous importance of the part played by the unconscious section of the human mind in determining behaviour. He invented psychoanalysis as a means of probing this hidden realm which he called the "Id". According to Freud's theory all our mental impulses were affected by "complexes" lodged in the Id; most of such complexes were determined by infantile sexuality. Religion, according to Freud, was simply an aberration like other mental abnormalities. He dismissed Christian belief, and the Jewish faith of his family, as "illusions" (8). The dictionary defines illusion as deceptive appearance or, false conception. In other words, "There is no God."

SCIENCE OR FANTASY?

Freud insisted that his beliefs and discoveries were founded on sound science; he taught that the techniques of psychoanalysis were as precise as the science of other branches of medicine. He laid down rules for the conduct of psychoanalysis: only those who themselves had been analysed could practice as analysts. He gathered around him a band of "disciples" all of whom had been analysed by him or by each other.

Freud's teaching was hailed with tremendous enthusiasm especially in the USA where he was said to have "changed the course of intellectual history" and to have influenced intellectuals more than any other modern thinker. Psychoanalysis, to its believers, solved all human problems (9). His theories must have been warmly welcomed in the ranks of secularists, humanists and atheists who could now claim scientific proof for their campaigns to abolish all restraints on human instincts imposed by Christian and other religions.

In criticising aspects of Freudian theory and practice I do not wish to take away the crucial benefit to patients of a sound doctor – patient relationship; in some cases, time must be found to explore the sensitive emotional factors as the cause of symptoms; this is not easy in the rush of NHS general practice but it can be achieved without formal psychoanalysis (10).

Freudian theory is a subject too vast to be pursued further here but the following comments are, I believe important:

The first is the irony of Freud's dismissal of God and religion when he himself was creating a new religion of psychoanalysis in which he took on the role of a Messiah! As mentioned above, Freud's technique of how the analyst deals with the patient is more a semi religious ritual than a thing of science. As in most religions, schisms occurred among psychoanalytic believers. Carl Jung and other followers, who disagreed with some aspects of Freud's teaching, founded their own brand of analysis, and attracted followers. The split in the Freudian ranks is reminiscent of what sadly seems to happen in most religions.

Secondly, there is no agreement in medical circles that analysis which involves, for the patient, endless hour long sessions, is successful as a cure. Opinions still differ on which treatment of mental or emotional illness is most effective – Freudian psychoanalysis or the use of powerful drugs.

Thirdly, in some cases, does psychoanalysis do more harm than good? The technique of analysis is supposed to bring to consciousness long repressed mental traumas, often associated with infantile or childhood parental relationships. Does this encourage the patient to blame his parents or siblings for all his or her present trouble and thus disturb family relationships?

Freud taught that much unhappiness and mental illness arose from the suppression of human instincts when a religious/class minority dominated the majority. He seemed to be advocating a free-for-all in sexual relationships and, in politics, a touch of Marxism. Did the embrace of Freud by academics in colleges of education, lead to serious decline in school teaching standards; and did his theory on loosening the "restraints on instincts" contribute to the upsurge of violence, vandalism and to the collapse of discipline?

Atheists might point out that in arguing for Christianity I am as guilty of the selective use of data as was Richard Dawkins in his argument against. The Christian response would, I hope, be agreement that in the last two thousand years there have been times when Christians did not adhere to the teaching of Christ; these failures will be discussed in chapter 11.

References

1. Barclay W. The Daily Study Bible, *Matthew vol 1, 7: 15-20.*

2. *Linner.,. Sex and Society in Sweden.* Jonathan Cape 1968.

3. *Catteral RD Interview,* GP, pp12,13, March 17 1972.

4. *Donald, Prof Ian. After the Pill: society under siege.* Daily Telegraph 10 April 1978.

5. *Barclay.W. The Daily Study Bible,* The Acts, p134. St Andews Press *Edinburgh, 1976.*

6. *Glubb Sir J.B. The Way of Love,* Hodder and Stoughton 1974.

7. *Bartholomew.J. The Welfare State we're in.* p13. Politio's Publishing 2004

8. *Freud Sigmund, The Future of an Illusion,* The Hogarth Press, London 1962.

9. *Rieff P. Freud: The mind of the Moralist.* Victor Gollancz 1960.

10. *Yellowlees W. All the world's a Stage* J, RCGP Supplement 3, vol XV11 1978

CHAPTER 9
BACK TO BASICS

Back to Basics in this chapter means going back to the Fertile
Crescent, that sweep of land from Egypt's Nile delta, through
Palestine to the lands bordering the rivers Tigris and Euphrates –
modern Iraq and Iran. In that Crescent, by 2000 BC, civilisation
had advanced far beyond the primitive darkness of human life in
other continents; the early invention of agriculture, some ten
thousand years ago, had enabled tribes of the Crescent to group into
nations with settled populations; for many centuries before 2000
BC, the farms and plantations, irrigated by the Nile in Egypt and in
Mesopotania by the Tigris and Euphrates had been exporting their
harvests far and wide; language, spoken or written on clay tablets or
papyrus, allowed trade between nations to flourish; learning and
literature were well developed (1).

Some nomadic tribes, still wandered with their flocks but
people in the Fertile Crescent, had emerged from the spiritual
darkness of hunter gathering; if civilisation was to progress, a code of
conduct which recognised good and evil was essential to protect
settled populations from reverting to savagery. Above all, the code
was required to protect and nourish that vital unit of nations, the
family, parented by husband and wife….. *for this reason a man will
leave his father and mother and be united to his wife, and they will
become one flesh.* (Genesis chap.2 :24)

According to the biblical account, on Mount Sinai, possibly
about 1400 BC, God revealed himself to his chosen twelve tribes,
the children of Israel; He gave to Moses, the leader of Israel, His Ten
Commandments which are the "Basics" of what we call civilisation.
The time and the exact location of Mount Sinai, are subject to
debate among biblical scholars (2). Here is a modern translation of
the Ten Commandments, published by the Lydia fellowship:

1. You shall have no other gods before me
2. You shall not make for yourself any carved image. You shall not
    bow down before them.
3. You shall not take the name of the Lord your God in vain.
4. Observe the Sabbath and Keep it Holy.

5. Honour your father and mother.
6. You shall not murder.
7. You shall not commit adultery.
8. You shall not steal.
9. You shall not bear false witness against your neighbours.
10. You shall not covet...anything that is your neighbour's.

SIMPLICITY

The virtue of the Ten Commandments is their supreme simplicity. The first four Commands deal with our relationship to God, the other six, with our relationship to each other. The details of human transactions with friends, neighbours, family, and environment can be infinitely complex, as are theories to explain human behaviour; but, as suggested in my introduction, basic *causes* of events can be simple. The late Lord Rutherford, one of the great architects of modern physics, believed that, *"if a theory is any good it should be understandable by an ordinary barmaid."* (3).

The Ten Commandments are not beyond the comprehension of a barmaid. Her customers, friends and family, might well understand, better than some academics and media pundits, that crime, violence, strife, adultery, murder, greed, envy would not flourish among people who strove to obey God's simple rules.

COMPLEXITY

The following comments on the Judaic Law of the Old Testament come from a gifted author and defender of Christianity, the late Douglas Reed. In the 1930s he worked for the London Times as correspondent in Central Europe. His popular books, *Insanity Fair,* and *Disgrace Abounding* warned readers of the threat from Nazi Germany and criticised the government for turning a blind eye to that threat.

From his experiences as a journalist, his travels and his contacts with leading European politicians, Reed had acquired a unique knowledge of political trends which, he believes, profoundly affect our lives today. In 1951 he embarked on a three year research stint in the USA to gather material for his book, *The Controversy of Zion*

(4). He worked mostly in the New York Central Library and also conferred with Jewish scholars, particularly a Dr. Kastein; for much of that time in New York he had to endure separation from his wife and young children. The following paragraphs give his views on the development of Judaic law which is relevant to the theme of *A Time to Weep*.

ISRAEL AND JUDAH

The history of the break-up of the former kingdom of Israel, mentioned in my introduction is important for our understanding of the New Testament. Douglas Reed elaborates on that history as follows:

Israel's ten northern tribes had been conquered by the Assyrians in 721 BC; the populations of those tribes could not all have been taken away into Assyrian slavery. Many must have remained while their families merged with surrounding peoples. The lands once occupied by the northern ten tribes of Israel included Galilee and Samaria whose people worshipped Jehovah but did not accept the supremacy of Judah. (As stated by the Samaritan women in her conversation with Jesus who had asked her for a drink of water from the well).

The tribes of Judah and Benjamin occupied the area of land forming the southern tip of what was once the kingdom of the twelve tribes of Israel; this small remnant, known as Judaea, on which stood the holy city of Jerusalem, was not conquered by the Assyrians in 721 BC. For centuries before 721, enmity had smouldered between Judah in the south and the northern ten tribes. After the death of King Solomon, Judah and Israel were completely separated and sometimes at war with each other

THE PENTATEUCH

As described in chapter 7, in BC 596, king Nebuchadnezzar's army conquered Judaea and deported many Judahites to Babylon; in captivity, as we have seen, they prospered and the Levites set to work in writing four books, Genesis, Exodus, Leviticus, and Numbers (5).

With the earlier-composed Deuteronomy, the five books are known as the Pentateuch, or Torah.

In BC 671, before their captivity, the Levites had completed the earliest writing of a book of the Old Testament, the book of Deuteronomy; they had read it out in the temple. Their claim that the statutes and instructions of the Pentateuch came to them directly from Jehovah via Moses is disputed by the US Jewish scholars, interrogated by Douglas Reed; they believed that much of the Pentateuch laws reflected, not the will of God, but that of the power-hungry Levites who made up laws to suit their own views and policies. Deuteronomy was more a political than a theological document. It contradicted the theme of the ten commandments by preaching not love and neighbourliness but racial superiority of the Jews over all other peoples. God would ensure conquest of gentile nations and the execution of their kings by the Jewish master race; racial purity forbade inter-marriage with gentiles; mixed marriages and apostasy would incur the death penalty.

The fate of Sihon, King of Heshbon, as described in Deuteronomy chapter 2, is an example of the law in action: *...We struck him down, together with his sons and his whole army...we took all his towns and completely destroyed them – men women and children. We left no survivors. But the livestock and plunder from the town we had captured we carried them off for ourselves.* A strange contradiction of the law against mixed marriages is the ruling that if a soldier of Judah sees an attractive women among pagan prisoners of war, he can take her to his home presumably as wife or concubine.

PERSIAN CONQUEST

In 559 BC the Persians conquered Babylon; although the Persain king, Cyrus, allowed any Judahites who so wished, to return to their home land, many stayed in Babylon. In 458 BC, Ezra, of the high priesthood came to Jerusalem from Babylon with some 1500 followers; he was dismayed to find widespread intermarriage between Jews and neighbouring peoples, so he assembled the people of Jerusalem and told them that all mixed marriages were to be dissolved; all "strangers" were to be excluded. Neighbouring peoples became alarmed at this unwelcome ruling which wrecked their peaceful, friendly relationships with the tribe of Judah; fearing for their security, they attacked Jerusalem and destroyed its walls; but after Ezra had returned to Babylon mixed marriages resumed.(6)

ANOTHER TIME TO WEEP

By 444 BC under the leadership of Nehemiah, assisted by his Persian masters, repairs to the walls of Jerusalem had been successfully accomplished; on a day, probably in that year, he arranged for the people to assemble in the square by the Jerusalem Water Gate. The prophet, Ezra, speaking from a high platform read out loud the book of the law: *...and the Levites who were instructing the people said to them all "This day is sacred to the Lord your God. Do not mourn or weep." For all the people had been weeping as they listened to the words of the law.* (Nehemiah, chap 8:v9)

Debate about Old Testament events of which records are scarce, bring uncertainty about dates and the relationship between Nehemiah and Ezra; much has to be guess work. Why, for that audience, was this a time to weep? I have asked this question to several authorities and been given three possibilities: a) Tears flowed because the Judahites, on hearing the law, realised their past sinfulness and were filled with remorse. b) They were moved to tears of ecstatic joy on hearing God's commands. Or, c) Douglas Reed suggests that their weeping expressed their sorrow when they realised that mixed marriages were now forbidden; husbands and wives would have to separate. Existing friendly relationships with neighbouring peoples would come to an end; they were entering a spiritual captivity which segregated all those of Jewish descent from other peoples. Fear of idolatry as well as the need for racial purity must have played a part in the forced segregation of Judah.

In verse 12 of the same chapter of Nehemiah (chap.8) we read that after their weeping: *Then all the people went away to eat and drink; to send portions of food and to celebrate with great joy, because they now understood the words that had been made known to them.* Did their tears turn into celebration with great joy "on the first day of the seventh month", because the reading of the law coincided with the Feast of Tabernacles (similar to our Harvest Festival), a time of great rejoicing and thankfulness for harvests gathered in?

THE RISE OF THE PHARISEES

Whatever caused the Jerusalem audience to weep on that day, there is no doubt that this remnant of God's people was starting a new phase in their history. The sect of the Pharisees followed the Levites in imposing a fanatical regime, the rules of which, according to Douglas Reed, resembled the 20th century communist manifesto. As well as strict racial segregation the new law encouraged people to report to the priestly authorities the names of anyone, even near relatives, seen to be disobeying the Pharisaic regime – a feature of modern secular dictatorships. For certain offences the death penalty remained; one such offence would occur....*If there arise among you a prophet or a dreamer of dreams...he shall be put to death* (Deut.13).

Until the coming of Jesus, the only significant group in Jerusalem who did not approve of Pharisaic dictatorship belonged to another priestly sect, the Sadducees; but the Pharisees remained dominant; their message included the promise of the Messiah who, they believed, would lead the campaigns of victorious conquest against all nations.

The inevitable confrontation with Jesus (was he seen by the Judah authorities *as a prophet or a dreamer of dreams?)* is told with graphic detail in the Gospels. In chapter 22 of his Gospel, Matthew tells how the Pharisees *laid plans to trap him in his words* by asking, *is it right to pay taxes to Caesar or not?* The famous reply of Jesus completely defeated their plan; *they were amazed. So they left him and went away.* (v.25)

They regrouped (v34) and one of the Pharisees, an expert in the law, asked Jesus '*which is the greatest commandment?'*. He replied that all the Law and Prophets depend on two Commandments; the first is '*Love the Lord your God with all you heart and with all your soul and with all your mind',* the second is '*Love you neighbour as yourself',* a reply which reflects the simplicity of the Ten Commandments and the futility of endless man-made regulations.

The attempts of the "experts" to trap Jesus in this argument is continued in Luke's gospel (chap10. vv 25-37) which tells how another '*expert in the law stood up to test Jesus'* by asking him the same kind of question as above. When the expert got the same reply including '*Love your neighbour as yourself*' he '*wanted to justify himself*', i.e. to show how clever he was in tripping up Jesus, by asking '*and who is my neighbour?*'

The reply of Jesus – *The Parable of the Good Samaritan* – is as powerful as a boxing knock out blow. The over-confident expert, totally defeated, had to admit that the Jewish priest and Levite had failed the neighbour test; the hero, a hated Samaritan, an enemy from the days of the Old Testament, had indeed acted with unselfish love and in so doing had demonstrated priestly hypocrisy and the futility of laws extolling racial superiority.

These encounters between Jesus and legal experts make clear why the Pharisees would not tolerate this popular Gallilean whose words and deeds attracted thousands of followers; they were determined to kill Him; He knew that his fate on the cross was inevitable, and that the events of the crucifixion and resurrection would "draw all men to him."

CONTROVERSY CONTINUED

When, following the resurrection of Jesus, Peter and John brought about miraculous healing in His name and boldly preached the message of the risen Christ as the saviour of the world, many of the people became believers. The Sanhedrin met in consternation and anger; they arrested Peter and John and put them in prison. They had to meet again when their prisoners miraculously escaped and continued to preach in the name of Jesus; once more the apostles were brought before the Sanhedrin and chief priests, some of whom urged execution of the prisoners. But a Pharisee called Gamaliel stood up and gave two examples of subversive characters who had attracted followers, had been put to death and were soon forgotten; he said: '*I advise you.. let them go. For if their purpose or activity is of human origin, it will fail. But if it is from God, you will not be able to stop these men; you will only find yourselves fighting against God*' (Acts Ch5: v 35). The Sanhedrin took this advice and released Peter and John.

The events following the Crucifixion, Resurrection and Pentecost, as told in the Book of Acts, have sometimes been described as a "spiritual explosion," a force which was to convert the

Roman empire to Christianity and to send inspired saints and martyrs far and wide so that within a few centuries Christianity became the foundation of European civilisation based on the Ten Commandments.

REFERENCES

1. Keller. W. *The Bible as History.* Hodder and Stoughton, 1956
2. Bright John, *A History of Israel* SCM Press London 1960.
3. Cleave T.L. *The Saccharine Disease.* Preface v, John Wright & Son Bristol 1975.
4. Reed Douglas. *The Controversy of Zion* Dolphin Press (Pty) Durban S. Africa 1978.
5. Ibid.
6. Ibid

CHAPTER 10
THE FALL OF JERUSALEM
SAUL OF TARSUS

The Sanhedrin took the advice of Gamaliel; they freed Peter and John from prison, but ignored his opinion that these two disciples of Jesus might be expressing, not the transient whim of a man, but the will of God; so, instead of quiet consideration of the matter, the Pharisees launched a campaign to root out and, if they thought it necessary, to kill the followers of Jesus, soon to be called Christians. One of the foremost Jewish persecutors, Saul of Tarsus, now enters the New Testament story as a vigorous young Pharisee. He had come to Jerusalem to stamp out this Jesus sect whose followers, inspired by the events of the first Easter, were growing in number; in particular, he came to deal with Stephen who had fearlessly accused the Sanhedrin of betraying and murdering Jesus Christ, the Messiah.

Saul played a leading role in the arrest and stoning to death of Stephen. As witnesses began hurling stones at the accused, they '*laid their clothes at the feet of a young man named Saul*'; then, as Stephen died a martyr's death, we are told in Acts 8:v11, '*And Saul was there giving approval to his death*'.

Years after his dramatic conversion when he encountered the risen Christ on the road to Damascus, and after his experiences as a leader of the missionaries who brought Christianity to Asia Minor, Greece and Rome, Saul, now called Paul, wrote to his young protégé, Timothy: '*In fact, everyone who wants to live a godly life in Christ Jesus will be persecuted*' (2 Timothy 3:12). In AD 60 or thereabouts when Paul wrote his letter to Timothy, the Jewish populations were far larger, as a Diaspora of 4.5 million throughout the Roman Empire, than the relatively small (one million) population of Judea. In Egypt alone, the Jews numbered about a million (1).

Scattered Jews with their synagogues were seen by the Roman authorities as useful, wealthy, and confident communities having an enviable reputation of stable family life; many were Roman citizens (2). According to Douglas Reed they remained segregated under strict Pharisaic control (3). The book of Acts certainly portrays

Jewish communities as active proselytes of the Jewish faith; hence their fierce, sometimes violent attacks on Paul and his companions where ever they preached the Gospel. Jewish authorities saw the growth of the early Christian church as a threat to the spread of Judaism; so the main persecutors of anyone who *wants to live a godly life in Jesus Christ',* at that time, were Jewish leaders who fomented the anti-Christian riots, (recorded by Luke, the "beloved physician" in the book of Acts.)

New Jewish laws, collectively known as the Talmud, composed at this time as an addition to the Torah, attempted to counter the Christian threat; it forbade the name of Jesus ever, under any circumstances, to be uttered or written(4).

Paul's example to Christians that they should expect imprisonment, persecution or martyrdom as the joyful privilege of belonging to the Christian church, encouraged rather than deterred new converts; the growth and success of churches throughout the Roman Empire during the two centuries following the events, described above, culminated in the Edict of Milan in AD 313 whereby full recognition was given to Christianity by the emperor Constantine and his co-emperor Licinius (5). In 320, although he did not altogether abandon his pagan gods, Constantine himself converted to Christianity and by AD1000 Christianity had become the foundation of European civilisation. After the long years of argument, schisms, and fierce academic disputes among the leaders of the early church, their agreement in AD367, on the choice of writings to be included in the final canon of the Bible is surely a miracle.

FINAL REVOLT

In Judea, some thirty years after the crucifixion of Jesus, Jewish hostility towards the Roman government erupted into four years of violent insurrection; here were the events, foreseen by Jesus, which had moved him to tears as he looked down on Jerusalem; they are events which bear an uncanny reminder of what is happening in Palestine today:

'Zealots roamed the country districts. Religious terrorism increased in the towns. The crowded processions of the great feasts became

occasions for sudden murders which provoked riots and brutal retaliation. Law and order broke down and Rome was blamed for the economic distress which ensued...The final revolt and its repression lasted four years. It placed a great strain on the military and economic resources of the empire and Rome was correspondingly vengeful' (6). The obvious difference between then, and what is now happening in the Middle East, almost two thousand years later, is the use, in the earlier conflict, of daggers and swords rather than high explosives! As Jesus had warned, the temple was destroyed when, in AD 70, Jerusalem was attacked by Roman troops. *'The Jewish nation never recovered from the blow, though the final dispersion took place in the next century, when Jerusalem was razed and rebuilt as a Roman colonial city'* (7).

MOVING GOVERNMENT

The priestly ruling council of Judea, having moved from Jerusalem, shortly before the city's destruction, settled in Jamnia, a town on the coast of Palestine. From there it continued to elaborate the Jewish law and to impose on the Jewish groups, still scattered all over the Roman Empire, strict obedience to the Pharisaic rule; the Law became the only agent which now held together the landless Jews, a nation in exile. We are told by Reed that thereafter, this movable headquarters was able to maintain strict control of its Jewish subjects as it moved, after about one hundred years in Jamnia, to Usha in Galilee; from Galilee it returned to the colony of Jews still in Babylonia; there, in the cities of Sura and Pumbedia Jewish academies were established; the leading academics and Rabbis, now known as Gaomins, maintained rule over all Jewish settlements (8).

THE MOVE TO EUROPE

After some six hundred years in the Middle East, the Gaomin/Sanhedrin Jewish government officials were able to establish their headquarters in mainland Europe. As camp followers of the forces of Islam, they travelled westwards through North Africa to Spain. The Moors, like the BC Babylonians and Persians, evidently had no objection to the Jews in their midst who now set up their government headquarters in Cordova, Spain; in time, the Spaniards realised that political interference seemed to be as much in the hands of Jewry as of Islam. Thus, when in 1492 the Spanish completed their expulsion of the Moors, the Jews also were expelled(9).

Where now would the mobile headquarters of Zionists find security? The surprising answer is: among the Khazar Jews in Poland. The Khazars are a unique example of a whole tribe who, without any ancestral roots in Palestine, nor any trace of Semitic blood, around the seventh century AD, converted en masse to the Jewish religion. Their story was told by Arthur Koestler in his book *The Thirteenth Tribe*. In the hope of refreshing my memory of this book I asked a local bookseller if it was available. The title was confirmed but the book seemed to have disappeared. Conspiracy theories should be viewed with caution, but is it not strange that in my copy of Chamber's Biographical Dictionary, published in 1975, among the list of books written by Koestler, *TheThirteenth Tribe* is not mentioned. Did this omission occur because, in the aftermath of World War Two, waves of immigrant Jews to the new state of Israel included many Khazars? The presence of the latter, who had no racial nor territorial claim whatsoever, might have weakened the Jewish case for a homeland in Palestine.

The governing body of Jewry had gone to Poland, but the mass of Jews, expelled from Spain and Portugal, whose descendents are labelled "Sephardic Jews" settled in many countries, Southern France, Italy, North Africa, Holland, England, Germany, Denmark and North and South America (10).

According to *The Controversy of Zion*, the Zionist "Government" seems to have moved from Poland to Russia where Jews played a prominent role in fomenting the Communist revolution of 1917. Thereafter, although the record is obscure, Douglas Reed suggests that the Jewish/Zionist power established itself in the USA.

THE ORIGIN OF STRIFE

Data in the following four paragraphs. is from
http:www.palestinerenenbered.com/Acre/Palestine-
Remembered/Story564.html

To return to Jerusalem, destroyed by the Romans around 132 AD. By 330 AD, Jerusalem became Christianised under Byzantine rule, only to be occupied in 638 AD by Islamists spreading out from Arabia; they built the Dome of the Rock in Jerusalem; by AD 750 the Holy City with its Christian churches and sepulchre was occupied by Moslems; predominately Arabic people now occupied the land of Judea... In 1099 Christian Europe responded to the Moslem conquest by launching a series of crusades in attempts to win back the Holy Land. After hard won victories, a Christian kingdom founded in Jerusalem lasted for about a century, but in 1187, Saladin launched a holy war against the Christians; his army forced the surrender of Jerusalem; so the land of the Christian/Judaic Bible again fell to the Moslems. Kings Henry IV and V of England dreamed of another Crusade to rescue Jerusalem for Christendom but quarrels between France and England destroyed any hope of a new united European expedition.

In 1516 the land of Palestine became part of the Turkish Ottoman Empire with its capital in Istanbul and remained so until 1918 when British troops commanded by General Allenby, assisted by the Lawrence of Arabia's irregulars triumphed over the Turks and entered Jerusalem.

THE BRITISH MANDATE

In 1917, the British Secretary of State, Mr. Balfour, had pledged British support for "a Jewish National Home in Palestine". Influential Zionists such as Baron Edmund de Rothschild had for many years been advocating the establishment of Jewish settlements in Palestine; he started financial backing for the proposal in 1882. A few years later, a Jewish Colonization Association was founded in

London and in Basle, Switzerland, the World Zionist Organisation also came in being.

When given the Mandate for Palestine in 1923, Great Britain faced the unenviable task of trying to keep the peace between the waves of Jewish immigrants, and the resident Arab populations who passionately believed that the land, which for generations they had cultivated, was theirs to keep. Our unfortunate soldiers and Palestine Police came under attack from both sides.

Strife in Palestine brings more questions than answers. How do neutral onlookers view the conflict between Jews and Arabic Palestinians, perpetuated by ongoing murder, destruction and occasional open warfare? That sentence was written some three weeks ago (June 30th, 2006) before our TV News showed tragic pictures from Palestine of destruction and death. Lebanon is being bombarded by Israeli artillery shells and by air craft, in retaliation for the capture by Hezbollah of two of Israel's soldiers and for their rocket attacks on Israel launched from Lebanon.

UNENDING VIOLENCE

As wave after wave of Jewish immigrants landed in Palestine in the 1920s and 30s violent disturbances by angry Palestinians caused many casualties, 5 Jews were killed and 200 wounded in 1920; then in 1921, during more protests against Zionist immigration, Palestinians killed 46 Jews and wounded 146. A Commission of enquiry attributed the trouble to the non fulfilment of a promise to give independence to Palestinian Arabs and their fear of political and economic consequences of Zionism.

At this time Zionists founded Haganah, an illegal underground military organisation. Later, in 1931 dissidents from Haganah, seeking more militant activity against Palestinians founded Irgun Zvai Leumil (National Military Organisation), Irgun or IZL for short. In 1939, yet another dissident Zionist group led by Avraham Stern, became known as the "Stern Gang" which received military support from Nazi Germany in order to terrorise the British Mandate.

Ninety-one people, including British and Jewish civil servants and their visitors, were killed in 1946 when a bomb, placed by

Irgun, blew up a wing of Jerusalem's King David Hotel, which was used as a base for the Mandate government.

PARTITION REJECTED

In 1947, proposals that Palestine should be partitioned between Zionists and Palestinians were fiercely resisted by the Arab League which had created the Arab Liberation Army to fight against partition. In the same year Britain recommended that the Mandate be terminated and a year later, in April 1948 came a climax of violence as Palestinian villagers fled from widespread Zionist offensives; the Stern Gangs massacred 250 people in the village of Dayr Yasin near Jerusalem; this and other Zionist attacks drove 200,000 Arab refugees from their homes and lands, soon to be occupied by immigrant Jews.

There is no space here to detail the sad account of subsequent Israel/Arab wars of the 1950s and 60s by which the Israelis have enlarged the area of land occupied by Jews and increased the number of Palestinian refugees. For countless Palestinian Arab and Jewish families, here is *A Time to Weep*; repeated peace-making attempts by international bodies have failed.

THE END OF THE PROMISED LAND

Christians, familiar with the Old Testament account of God's promise to give to the Hebrews the land, "flowing with milk and honey," may sympathise with the Zionists searching for a Jewish homeland; and we cannot forget the terrible suffering of the Jews, persecuted, imprisoned and slaughtered in WWII by Hitler's Nazis.

To understand the conflict of today we must go back to 130 AD, the year of the *final dispersion*, described above under the heading *Final Revolt*. History does not tell us of any official persecution, suffered by the Jews scattered throughout the Roman Empire; indeed as noted above, Jewish communities were valued for their stability; Rome's ruling arm reacted with severity only if imperial peace was threatened by violence. In Judea the Sadducees and others preferred the rule of Rome to that of their own leaders. If no specific oppression is evident as the cause of the four years of insurrection by Jewish terrorists, why had law and order broken down amid violence, terrorism and murder? The only possible answer is the Zionist racial fanaticism, later expressed in the new Talmudic law: '*Thou shalt reign over every other nation, but they shall not reign over thee*'. To the Zionist authors of this command, Roman rule, however benevolent, was intolerable; they eagerly expected the coming of the Messiah who would lead the armies of God's chosen people in wars to triumph over *every other nation*. Paul Johnson suggests that some members of the Jerusalem wing of the early Christian church reverted to Judaism and supported the insurgency against Rome.

From the four years of violence, murder and terrorism came an outcome which totally defeated the Zionist aims. Rome lost patience and having razed Jerusalem to the ground established the place as a Roman colonial city; Jews were further dispersed, a situation for which the Zionists had no one but themselves to blame.

It is beyond the scope of *A Time to Weep* and beyond the scholarship of its author to adequately comment on Douglas Reed's belief that the hidden power of the Zionist network, ultimately centred in the USA, worked, through the centuries, to accomplish the return of Jews to Palestine and the triumph of Zion *to reign over every other nation*.

Lest I be accused of anti-Semitism, I wish to aver that during my career as an NHS GP some of my most valued friends have been Jews whose skills and abilities have contributed greatly to medical and other sciences. We never discussed religion or politics but none of my Jewish friends seemed to be Zionists.

References

1. Johnson Paul *A history of Christianity p11,* Penguin Books London 1978
2. Ibid
3. Reed Douglas *The Controversy of Zion* Dolphin Press (Pty) Durban S. Africa 1978.
4. Ibid
5. Johnson Paul, *A History of Christianity* p67 Penguin Books. London, 1978.
6. Ibid p42
7. Ibid
8. Reed Douglas *The Controversy of Zion* Dolphin Press (Pty) Durban S.Africa, 1978.
9. Ibid p 83 .
10. Ibid.

CHAPTER 11
THE PROMISED LAND AND ISLAM
LEBANON DISASTER

The media news today, 27th July 2006, continues to feature dreadful images from the country traditionally known as the "Holy Land". Hezbollah rockets, fired at Israel from Lebanon, are answered by Israeli air force bombs and ground artillery shells which rain down on residential streets, houses and flats of the towns of southern Lebanon; day after day our TV screens show awful scenes of destruction, blood and death. Some of the thousands of terrified refugees seek safety on ships coming on rescue missions to Palestine's sea ports. Escape is made all the more difficult and dangerous by the destruction of roads and bridges by Israeli air force bombers – surely *A Time to Weep.*

We are told by radio and television of high-level meetings, as diplomats shuttle to and fro between Palestine, the U.S White House, Westminster and the UN. Amid the wringing of hands and hectic discussions on how to end the bloodshed, very few commentators seem to be aware of the early history of the Arab/Zionist conflict.

EARLY HISTORY

The following facts are seldom, if ever, mentioned:

1. In the first century AD, after the destruction of Jerusalem by the Romans, a final dispersal left only a tiny remnant of Jews in Palestine (1).

2. Between 1882 and 1914 a total of some 65,000 Jewish immigrants, many from eastern Europe, arrived in two separate landings which increased the Jewish fraction of the Palestine population to about 6.5% of the total. (2).

3. A third wave of 35,000 immigrants between 1919 and 1922 raised the Jewish percentage to 12%, but in 1923 only 3% of

the land area of Palestine was registered as in Jewish ownership. In October of that year (1922) the first British census of Palestine showed that out of a total population of 757,182, the percentages of the three racial groups were: Muslim Arab 78%, Jewish 11%, Christian Arab 9.6% (3).

In other words, for almost two thousand years, Arabs were by far the largest ethnic group in the land of Palestine. Opinions seem to differ on the reaction of the Arabs to these waves of Jewish immigration; a speaker in a recent radio discussion suggested that some Arab residents were content to sell portions of their land to the incomers; but surely the main thrust of Arab resentment has been the forceful seizure of land by Jewish settlers, protected by a large powerful Israeli army which could never have been recruited, trained and equipped without massive help from the USA.

BIBLICAL TEXTS

A few months ago, a brief TV News item dealing with the Palestinian conflict, showed a middle-aged Zionist, brandishing a Bible and declaring "*the Bible is our justification*" or words to that effect. Certainly the first five books of the Bible dwell on God's promise to give that area of land, later known as Palestine, to the "Children of Israel" who, if they kept God's commands, would achieve the status of a master race, able to rule over all other races, a goal which, according to the book of Deuteronomy, can be achieved by the conquest, destruction and indiscriminate slaughter of gentiles. However, the strictures of the prophets, expressed in the later books of the Old Testament, quoted in my introduction, suggest that the chosen race, through the disobedience, corruption, and avarice of its leaders, may have lost God's favour. The Bible reader might also do well to turn to the New Testament and to read the parable of the *Vineyard Tenants* as spoken by Jesus (Matthew, ch. 21, vv 33-41). For readers unfamiliar with this parable, here is a brief summary:

A land owner planted a vineyard, and because he had to go away on a journey, rented it to tenants; at harvest time he sent servants to the vineyard to harvest his fruit. The servants were beaten up, stoned or killed, by the tenants. The same thing happened to a larger squad of servants, sent by the landowner, who then said, '*I will send my son, they will respect him*'. But the tenants, recognising the son, said to each other '*let's kill him and take his inheritance*'; so they threw the son out of the vineyard and killed him. As in the parable of the Good Samaritan, having told the story, Jesus asks his listeners a crucial question, in this case: '*when the owner of the vineyard comes, what will he do to those tenants?*'

> '*He will bring those wretches to a wretched end*' they replied '*and he will rent the vineyard to other tenants who will give him his share of the crop at harvest time*'....

The obvious identity of the characters does not infer permanent Zionist occupation of the vineyard (the Holy Land) by the tenants (the Jews and their leaders) who have assaulted the owner's servants (the Prophets) and murdered his son (Jesus, the Messiah).

We are not told by Matthew whether Jesus agrees with the audience's response that God will rent the vineyard to other tenants; he simply says to them: '*Have you never read the scripture: the stone that the builders rejected has become the corner stone.*' The future ownership of the Promised Land can best be understood when we realise that, in this parable, the vineyard does not stand only for earthly territory, but for the spiritual Kingdom of God in which the Son of God, rejected and murdered, becomes the most important person in the world(4).

THE KINGDOM OF GOD

In an other of his books, The Mind of Jesus (5), the late Professor William Barclay devotes a chapter to the meaning of *The Kingdom of God*; he lists the necessary qualifications of those who seek entry to the Kingdom, and explains the difficult concept of a spiritual Kingdom which exists in the past, present and future. Obstacles in the way of entering the Kingdom feature in the gospels, for instance, while material wealth is not a sin, entry can be difficult for a rich person. Jesus himself is the unique embodiment of the Kingdom; He brings to humanity the message of obedience to the will of God the Father; He is the shining example of humility, mercy and concern for those who suffer from poverty, oppression or sickness.

Having endured and triumphed in the desert over Satan's temptations, Jesus returned to Galilee and embarked on a mission of teaching in synagogues;...*news of him spread through the whole countryside....and everyone praised him* (Luke 4:10)

Professor Barclay gives a revealing interpretation of Luke's account of the first occasion on which Jesus spoke in the synagogue of his family's hometown, Nazareth. According to custom at the Sabbath services, during which any of the congregation could read a passage of scripture and speak, Jesus was handed the scroll of the prophet Isaiah. The following paragraph is taken from the professor's book, mentioned above (6).

There is a curious, deliberate finality in the way in which Luke tells how Jesus read this passage. He read this great promise of the mercy of God, and then, he closed the book (Luke 4:20). If that is so, then Jesus actually stopped in the middle of the verse as the verses are arranged in the English version of Isaiah. He stopped half way through Isaiah 61.2. And what follows? At what does Jesus stop? He stops at the words *'to proclaim the day of vengeance of our God'*. That part of the prophesy Jesus did not read. We can only think that he stopped there because he did not regard that as his task; it was mercy, not vengeance, that he came to offer men; it was love not wrath. He is above and beyond all else the messenger of mercy.

A GOD OF VENGEANCE

The refusal of Jesus to declare himself to be a God of vengeance brings us back to the Controversy of Zion, and to contrasts between some parts of the Old Testament and the message of Jesus. The book of Deuteronomy depicts the God of the Old Testament as being the spiritual ruler of a world-wide Jewish kingdom where vengeance, and severe punishment will be the fate of all peoples who do not bow down and obey laws, some of which (according to Douglas Reed) came, not from the mind of Jehovah, but from the power-hungry Levites, then later from the 'Scribes and Pharisees'.

Today, 7th August 06, a ceasefire has mercifully been obeyed in Lebanon and Israel; actions of vengeance by both antagonists have for the moment ceased but bitter hostility remains. What should be the attitude of a Christian, weeping as he or she watches from the sidelines this unending conflict over the Promised Land; where lies the blame? In the 20th century, the seizure by Israel of lands, occupied for generations by Arabs, was bound to provoke a violent response. That response has repercussions far beyond Palestine and may continue to have profound world-wide consequences for years to come. So much of what goes on in the corridors of power is hidden that we can only express our fears and hopes by asking questions:

A)   Is the failure to find a peaceful solution to the Israeli/Arab conflict over the territory of Palestine the central, fundamental cause of most of the unrest, warfare, and terrorism which now, all over the world, blights the lives of peace loving peoples?

B)   Islamists identify the USA government as the force behind Zionist aggression in the Holy Land, and they see British foreign policy closely linked to that of the US. Is this assumption correct?

C)   Were the objectives of the invasion of Iraq in 2002, partly to secure oil supplies, but mostly to protect Israel from the rockets of Saddam Hussein?

How much of the latter objective resulted from Zionist pressure within the US Government?

The Zionist with his bible is not alone in quoting from the Old Testament in support of the claim of racial superiority. Muslims believe that the Pentateuch or Torah comprises one of the four sacred books of law by which Allah revealed his commands to mankind. Thus, in their claims to racial superiority, supported by a God of vengeance against all who do not share their religion, Zionists and Muslims can quote from the same Old Testament rule book; in Islamic nations, the punishment for apostasy is still the death penalty.

I have not studied the Koran in detail, but am indebted to the writings of Patrick Sookhdeo, International Director of the Barnabus Fund, for his knowledge of Islamic literature and Shariah or religious law by which, in Islamic countries, non-Muslim minorities, especially Jews and Christians are treated as inferior, subjugated people whom Muslims name dhimmi (7).

CHRISTIAN MINORITIES

Reports to the Barnabas Fund of continuing subjugation and persecution of Christian minorities living in Islamic nations gives harrowing images of suffering and cruelty; here are some examples:

Recently Uzbekistan celebrated the 15th Anniversary of independence. During the month of August 2006, Christian church leaders and their families have been deported without any reason or court order. Christian women and children have been beaten, funds raised for Christian activity confiscated.

In the Punjab region of Pakistan, Christian children aged between six and twelve are being abducted from their homes and held in appalling conditions where they are beaten and then sold for $1,700 each into the sex trade or servitude. Two brave missionaries; one Pakistani, one British managed to buy back 20 boys from this wicked slave trade and to identify its manager, Ghul Khan. Such is the power of this individual that the Pakistani authorities have refrained from arresting him (8).

In February of 2006, in response to the Danish cartoon depicting the prophet Muhammad, a Nigerian mob killed fifty Christians; thirty Nigerian Christian churches were burned down. During a similar violent protest, in Iraq, four Christian churches were bombed, and in Pakistan six Christian schools and a Christian hospital were attacked (9).

In Somalia, Christians are a very small fraction of a predominantly Muslim population; there, a college student who converted from Islam to Christianity was shot dead on 7th September 2006. In October 2005 a Christian Evangelist, a leader of a house church, was shot dead by Islamists. (10)

POPE BENEDICT'S LECTURE

It is uncanny how, as I try to write objectively on a complex and difficult subject, media headlines give a dramatic example of the Islam/Christian conflict. This morning's (16th September 06) radio news highlights the extraordinary Islamic reaction following a lecture given in Germany by Pope Benedict; during his lecture the Pontiff quoted from a book written in the 14th century which reports a conversation between a Byzantine Christian emperor and an educated Persian on the subject of a holy war. The offending words uttered by the emperor were:

"Show me just what Mohammed brought that was new, and there you will find things only evil and inhuman, such as his command to spread by the sword the faith he preached".

An hysterical world-wide Islamic outburst has erupted in the last 24 hours; effigies of the Pope have been publicly burned; my morning paper's front page carries a photograph of a crowd of fanatical gesticulating young Moslem men at a rally, held in Jammu, India. The most obvious comments by a neutral observer, are, firstly, that the offending words were conceived by a man living some six hundred years ago; Pope Benedict merely quoted them in the course of a lecture dealing with "faith and reason." Secondly, examples of Islamist violence and cruelty some of which are recorded in this chapter confirm that Islam is indeed "spread by the sword"; how else can we describe the slaughter in recent years of hundreds of innocent victims in Europe, Asia, the USA by Islamist bombers? We now know that some of the latter were British Muslims. The following paragraphs in italics come from the Barnabas Foundation email news of 5th September 2006.

BRITISH MUSLIM

Peter Clark, head of Scotland Yard Anti-Terrorist Branch, speaks of thousands of militant British Muslims, indoctrinated and radicalised in British mosques and madrassas like the Jameah Islameah school recently raided in Sussex. Islamic extremism has spread in Britain thanks to a particular brand of multiculturalism encouraged by this government. And until ministers tackle it – especially the influence of Muslim faith schools – their efforts to build cohesion will come to very little...

It might seem paradoxical that the UK, which has granted Muslims greater freedoms than any other Western country, should be the greatest incubator of Islamist violence. The explanation lies not only in the radicalisation of Islam but also in the Government's policy on multiculturalism... In West Ham a gigantic Mosque is planned by the radical Tablighi Jamaat group. The London Thames Gateway Development Corporation says that the new mosque will make West Ham a "cultural and religious destination". This will be nothing less than an Islamic quarter of our capital city.

I wonder if, in years to come, people will look back in amazement at the weakness of British governments during the decades following the 1945 allied victory over arrogant, wicked dictatorships. Hitler, backed by Mussolini's Fascists, launched his armed forces in the vain hope of conquering all Europe including the British Isles. How did it come about, that our frontiers, successfully defended, from 1939 on land, sea and in the air, through five long years of a harsh and terrible war, were thrown wide open to allow apparently uncontrolled and unrecorded entry into our country of immigrants, some thousands of whom (according to the Head of Scotland anti-terrorist branch) are bent on the destruction of our freedom and laws?

Our way of life was founded on Christianity, on the worship of a God of mercy, not of vengeance. In the past we have rightly welcomed to our land those genuinely fleeing from persecution. We allow freedom of speech and of worship; but if that freedom is threatened by in-comers, a minority of whom are intent on violence and murder, should we not demand, of those seeking British citizenship, an oath of loyalty to our country and a signed agreement to obey to our laws? The majority of British Muslims are peace-loving but are not some of their leaders bound by Sharia law which demands the taking over of our country until it is part of the Muslim empire? Such a religion which is more political than spiritual and is spread by the sword makes a mockery of multiculturalism.

Zionist and Muslim critics will be eager to respond with anger to the theme of this chapter by listing the failings, sins and cruelties of those professing, in the last two thousand years, to be Christians. In chapter 12, I will attempt to discuss such criticism.

REFERENCES

1. Johnson Paul, *A History of Christianity*, Penguin Books 1988
2. http:www.palestineremembered .com
3. Ibid.
4. Barclay W. *The Gospel of Matthew* vol 2. p 264, St.Andrew Press 1986
5. Barclay *The Mind of Jesus*, SCM Press 1978.
6. Ibid p66
7. Sookhdeo P. *Christian's Guide to Islam*. Christian Focus Publication 2002.
8. Barnabas Fund email news, Sept 06
9. Ibid
10. Ibid

CHAPTER 12
FORGIVE US OUR SINS

A writer, whose education required prolonged study of human physiology, pathology, histology, pharmacology, and other disciplines related to medicine, may justifiably, be criticised for venturing into realms of theology. So I ask for forgiveness if any of my statements in defence of Christianity are shown to be wrong. My use of the word 'Christianity' refers to the lives and the work of earth-bound believers who worship the transcendent God of the bible; they profess to be members of the Christian church and are motivated by the Holy Spirit, promised by Jesus.

In defending the Faith, it would be wrong and dishonest to omit examples of controversy through varying interpretation of scriptures. The writers of the New Testament Gospels did not attempt to cover up misunderstandings and faults among the Apostles who sometimes failed to grasp the teaching of Jesus; there were rivalries; one of the twelve betrayed Jesus and the rest, apart from Peter and John, fled when He was arrested in Gethsemane.

Throughout its history, the Christian church has been beset by schisms, faults, failures and sometimes violence; in the days of the Inquisition, in the name of Christianity, heretics were shown no mercy; they were persecuted, hunted down, tortured or killed for what to us were relatively trivial lapses. To quote from Paul Johnson: *The last official Spanish execution for heresy was in 1862, when a schoolmaster was hanged for substituting 'Praise be to God' in place of 'Ave Maria' in school prayers (1.)*

We must give thanks that in Europe these miseries are gone. As evidence of better, peaceful times, the recently published, most up-to-date, new international version of the Holy Bible has come to us, thanks to the agreement and skills of translators from the USA, Great Britain, Canada and New Zealand, representing all known denominations of the Reformed Church. Faced with texts written in Hebrew, Aramaic, and Greek these Christian translators, united in their conclusions in spite of their diversity, have given us the popular N.I.V. Some Christians may miss the wonderful Shakespearian cadences and archaic language of the King James Bible, passages of which they often had to learn by heart at school. But language does not stand still and the new translation has managed to clarify meaning while maintaining something of the style of the King James version.

CRUSADES

In their sometimes strident criticism of Christianity, Islamists seldom omit to remind us of the Crusades; they do so as if events, which began in the closing months of the eleventh century, had happened yesterday. As in the case of Northern Ireland today, were not the armed campaigns of the Crusades as much over *territory,* as over religion? The deep concern and anger felt by the nations of Christian Europe can be well understood, when, by the year AD 700, militant Muslims had occupied Jerusalem with its Christian Holy Sepulchre; but Jesus taught that His Kingdom was not of this world, and on both sides of that medieval conflict the lure of conquest, booty and adventure probably gave motives as strong as those of the spirit.

The sad fruits of the Crusades, apart from the wounds of battle, loss of lives, and ruinous expenditure of wealth, gave rise to a legacy of Muslim hostility towards Christian Europe; the Crusades also raise the endlessly difficult question for Christians: should they embrace pacifism or is war justified when unprovoked aggression threatens our way of life?

SCHISMS

Given the fallen nature of mankind, groups of human beings, brought together for any purpose including divine worship are prone to quarrels, differences, splitting off of minorities, individuals going off in a huff and so on. Alas! Christian congregations are not immune to these failings. I mentioned above the miracle of agreement on the choice of the final canon of the Christian Bible, in spite of the bitter disagreements and quarrels which occurred among the academic church leaders in the first two centuries AD.

It is of little comfort to remind Muslims that Christians of varied denominations may disagree in details of Christian ritual and worship, but they do not now emulate the violent sectarian Islamic warfare between Sunnis and Shiahs, recently highlighted by the slaughter of many Shiahs when a bomb was exploded in one of their mosques.

The saddest Christian schism came with the Reformation of the 16th century. Will that wound ever be healed? We can only pray that healing and understanding will progress and that the past differences will be gone forever in the hope of a new unity of Catholics and Protestants.

REMEMBER THE SABBATH

My father, David Yellowlees, born in 1874 in Stirling, as a young man acquired a bicycle; to try it out one Sunday afternoon, he peddled up what is now the A9 road to the village of Braco, some eight miles north of Stirling where a cousin toiled as a farmer. He was greeted thus: "David, we are glad to see you at any time, but not on a bicycle on the Sabbath!" So, in those Victorian days, there seemed to be no relaxation of the 18th century strictness of observance of the Scottish Sabbath. My father sometimes spoke of the misery of Sunday in those days when the joys of sport and recreation were forbidden. All secular literature was banished for the day; the funereal tone of this regime goes against the divine purpose of the seventh day of celebration and rest.

In Old Testament times, before the invention of machines, powered by fossil fuels or other sources of energy, almost all the energy, essential in settled communities for the production and distribution of food, clothing or shelter, had to come from the muscles of domesticated animals or the muscles of human beings. Regular weekly bodily rest for beasts and humans was necessary for the maintenance of muscular function.

The Industrial Revolution and the invention of ever more sophisticated machines brought profound change in the pattern of work and greatly relieved the need for muscular energy. As the use of muscle power declined, sedentary occupations increased. The huge armies of mechanics, tending their machines or millions of office-bound staff, stuck day after day at their desks, suffered deprivation of muscular effort. On the day of rest, what they needed was physical exercise for their bodies and rest for their nervous systems. (2)

In any case, was it not a mistake to confuse the Jewish Sabbath, a Saturday, with the Christian seventh day, Sunday, which celebrates the Resurrection of Jesus. The Christian Sunday should therefore be a day, not of misery, but of rejoicing, when Christians can meet at church to maintain and strengthen their faith with music, song and prayer and by their Pastor's interpretation of scripture. If they then went out to enjoy physical exercise by climbing hills, walking in the countryside, or playing ball games, would they be blamed for breaking the fourth Commandment? Jesus healed on the Sabbath.

But perhaps we have gone too far down the road to a secular Sunday. Should not shop-keepers and *professional* cricketers or footballers have their day of rest? (Might these professional players then be less liable to injury?). In the film *Chariots of Fire*, we were reminded of the life of that hero of Scottish athletics, Edinburgh University's Eric Liddell. He had been born in Tientsin, North China in 1902, the son of Scottish Christian missionaries.

In 1924 he was included in the British team for the Paris Olympics and when he learned that the heats for the 100 metres sprint were to be run on a Sunday, he quietly withdrew his name from that event. However, in the final of the 400 metres (not on a Sunday):

'He was pitted against the formidable H.M. Fitch of the United States and hope fell when it was seen that Liddell had drawn the outside lane. As the race proceeded, excitement rose to fever pitch and finally to a frenzy when Liddel burst into the home straight with a lead of four yards. At the tape, Liddel won by six yards from Fitch and the scenes of enthusiasm which greeted his victory were renewed when it was announced that his time 47.4 sec. was a world record.' (3)

Before the start of the race a small piece of paper had been handed to Liddell; on it was written: "Them that honoureth me, I will honour." (4) At the height of his athletic fame, Liddell returned to Tientisin; there, he continued the missionary work of his parents until the Japanese invaded during World War Two; in 1945 this devout Christian died in a Japanese prison camp.

THE DOUR SCOTS

My great, great, grand father, another David Yellowlees, born in 1752, worked a farm, Mountjoy, near the town of Linlithgow. He … *'was nominated as an elder of the kirk, but an objection was lodged, and a meeting of session was convened to consider the objection, which was this – "His wife had once danced at a wedding!" Needless to say the "wickedness" was not heinous enough to prevent his being ordained!'*(5)

No wonder the Scottish race have been caricatured as dour and mirthless, in view of their eighteenth century Presbyterian church regime in which church members could condemn an aspiring church elder, because his wife, my great, great, grand mother had danced at that wedding. (Her name was Mary Russell, born in 1754).

In those days, the elders of the Church of Scotland exercised much more authority and control over the behaviour of their members than they do today. The system of eldership has a long biblical tradition going back to the time of Moses. (Exodus Ch 24, v.1). Elders are appointed and given districts according to the number of members in each congregation; their duties are to look after and to serve their districts on behalf of the minister with whom they meet regularly as members of the Kirk Session. In the days of my dancing ancestor, no doubt some elders relished their role as moral bosses; music, dancing and frivolity on the part of church leaders were clearly not permitted.

A superb speaker from Paisley, the late William McCulloch created recitations in Scots Doric, recorded on gramophone records which were very popular in the 1930s. One recitation tells of a village church congregation whose elders were dismayed to be told that their minister had acquired and had been heard playing a fiddle! An emergency meeting of elders was called and a small deputation elected to visit the manse and to reprove the minister for fiddle playing.

The deputation was welcomed and shown into the sitting room to meet the minister's wife and a visiting aunt. The elders were amazed at the enormous size of the "fiddle" which the minister brought into the room. It was, of course a 'Cello; soon the elders were in raptures as their minister sat down and played some old Scots songs and psalm tunes; suddenly he changed the tempo and broke into the joyful tune of a Scottish reel. One elder jumped to his feet and 'grippet' the minister's wife, another 'grippet' the aunt and they launched into a foursome reel! As far as I can remember, on leaving the manse, the deputation decided that "Yon was a releegious fiddle".

Robert Burns whose somewhat erratic love life brought reproof from church elders took terrible revenge in his poem *Holy Willie's Prayer,* a masterpiece of satire. William Fisher, the subject of the poem, was a real person who has been identified as an elder of the church of Mauchline (Ayrshire); he exercised rigid supervision of his parishioners one of whom he reported for sending a servant to lift some potatoes from his garden on a Sunday. But Willie was well known for his heavy drinking and for the suspicion that his own relationships with the fair sex were not without blemish; it was also rumoured that he had pocketed some of the church funds! (6).

The Church of Scotland today is not, I hope, burdened with pompous 'Holy Willies'; the system of eldership encourages a team spirit which gives strength to congregations by supporting the minister at worship and in the manifold duties of running various church organisations. The problem now is not the rule of over-enthusiastic elders, it is to find volunteers to do the work – a problem reflected in the sad decline in Church membership during the second half of the 20th century. Here is an amateur theologian's choice of four factors which have brought about that decline.

1. The Pharisaic-like regimes of control, exemplified in the above paragraphs.
2. Darwin's *Origin of the Species* published in 1859, then, later in the writings of the Austrian doctor, mentioned in chapter 8, Sigmund Freud, creator of Psychoanalysis whose 'Magnum Opus' *The Interpretation of Dreams,* was published in 1900; he taught that all religions were simply illusions.
3. The rise of an academic establishment, influenced by Darwin and Freud, especially among the scientific fraternity, who scorned Christianity, many of whom embraced Humanism and Sectarianism.

4. The mostly awful standards of 'The Gutter Press' and of television programmes, for ever featuring themes of violence, murder and sex.

TRIUMPH, NOT DISASTER

Against these failures should be set the triumphs of Christianity whose missionaries brought the Good News of the Gospels from Palestine to Europe thence to the whole world. Christianity brought about the abolition of slavery, fostered universal education, care of the sick, stable family life, a law abiding climate, justice and above all, "Charity" in the biblical sense of that word, as proclaimed in ringing eloquence by St. Paul (7). Charity, better defined by the word, 'Love', has motivated countless Christians from congregations of all denominations world-wide, to work tirelessly by words and deeds for the relief of human suffering.

The work of church organisations such as the Women's Guilds, Boys Brigades, and many others goes on unsung; the Salvation Army year by year brings hope to the homeless and those deprived by poverty and the breakdown of human relationships.

The Latin word for charity, "Caritas" is used in the motto of the Royal College of General Practitioners: *Cum Scientia Caritas* (Along with Science, Loving Care.) Having been retired from the NHS for some twenty-five years, perhaps I am not qualified to comment on recent developments, but while in both hospitals and what is now called 'Primary Care,' *Scientia* goes from strength to strength, it is sad to hear of some patients being distressed for the want of a simple injection of *Caritas*.

Perhaps my attempt to give, in this chapter, a balanced account of the Christian Faith would not win approval from theologians; but the account would not be complete without exploring covert forces against the Faith to be discussed in the next chapter.

REFERENCES

1. Johnson Paul, *A History of Christianity p308* Penguin Books London 1975.
2. Barclay William, *The Plain Man's Guide to Ethics,* p 41, Fontana Books 1973.
3. Usher Col. C.M, *The Story of Edinburgh University Athletic Club.* T & A Constable, Edin. 1966.
4. Ibid p 65.
5. Yellowlees John, *The Yellowlees Family,* p.37, Neidpath Press, Peebles 1931
6. *The Poetical Works of Robert Burns*, p 563, Collins Clear-Type Press, publication undated.
7. Corinthians 1, Chap. 13, vv 1-13.

CHAPTER 13
THE NEW WORLD ORDER

'The world is governed by very different personages from what is imagined by those who are not behind the scenes'.

The statement, quoted above, is attributed to Benjamin Disraeli (1804-81). At the outset of his political career, he became well known as a writer of novels and went on to hold the office of Chancellor of the Exchequer and then Prime Minister; he was a favourite of Queen Victoria, on whom he conferred the new title of Empress of India. In 1878 at the Congress of Berlin, held to avoid the threat of an attack on Constantinople by the Russians, Disraeli's skills as a diplomat deeply impressed Germany's Bismark who was heard to declare, 'Der alte Jude, das ist ein Mann'. (*'The old Jew, that is a real man'*)

BEHIND THE SCENES

Who are those 'personages' who, according to Disraeli, secretly governed the world more than a hundred years ago; in spite of 'Freedom of Information,' are they still 'governing' the world today? They worked secretly, so must surely qualify as true conspirators. Theorists, who create conspiracies out of thin air, are rightly derided as fantasists; but the statement, quoted above, made by a politician, as gifted and experienced as Disraeli, deserves to be taken seriously, in the light of the dictionary definition of 'Conspiracy', *'Plot or plotting for evil.'*

In his book, *Europe's Full Circle*, Rodney Atkinson has published sensational evidence (1) on the activities of 'personages' working behind the scenes since the end of the first World War; he tells how their aim, to abolish sovereign nation states, and to establish a 'New World Order' was, and still is, powered by a group of distinguished intellectuals, influential politicians, global corporatists, bankers and financiers. One of these intellectuals, Arnold Toynbee, a well known scholar, historian and diplomat, worked in the Foreign Office, during both World Wars. As Director of Studies at The Royal Institute of International Affairs, Chatham House, London, he became a fervent advocate of a 'New World Order.'

Rodney Atkinson had difficulty in obtaining the full text of a paper delivered by Arnold Toynbee at the 1931 Royal Institute conference; when, at last, he persuaded the Institute to let him read the full text, Atkinson concluded that the paper revealed Toynbee as a 'wild, aggressive, nation hating, world government fanatic.' Here is one brief quote from Toynbee's 1931 paper: *'we are at present working discreetly but with all our might to wrest this mysterious political force called sovereignty out of the clutches of the local nation states of the world. And all the time we are denying with our lips what we are doing with our hands'.* (2) I have underlined the last sentence because it clearly reveals how certain 'New World Order' evangelists use duplicity to achieve their ends.

THE BILDERBERG GROUP

The following paragraphs on the activities of the Bilderberg Group are mostly taken from the above mentioned book by Rodney Atkinson who tells how the secret movement for the abolition of sovereign nation states, gained force after the second World War (3). A Polish Socialist, Joseph Retinger who seems to have had a genius for identifying prominent figures and persuading them to join his mission for a New World Order, played a leading role to this end, by enlisting the help of the German Prince Bernhard of the Netherlands who had joined Hitler's Nazi party in 1933. As an SS officer, Prince Bernard's duties included attachment to the Nazi party's chief industrial supporter, I.G.Farben, but on marrying the future Queen of the Netherlands in 1937, he had to resign from the Nazi party. In 1954, deeply influenced by Retinger, and assisted by Paul Rykens the then Chairman of Unilever, Prince Bernard managed to gather together, in Holland, a large crowd of leading politicians, industrialists, Bankers, media pundits, journalists and others, from the US, Europe and the Commonwealth; this assembled sample of the world's most influential leaders took place in the Bilderberg hotel in the town of Oosterbeek, Holland; hence the name of the group.

Since its birth in 1954, secrecy has shrouded the Bilderberg Group's annual meetings, held in large, top class hotels which are totally booked for several days and stringently surrounded by armed guards. Press journalists, who eagerly seek scoops to reveal the intimate secrets of politicians, actors, sports persons, royalty, or other celebrities, are evidently successfully muzzled at the Bilderberg meetings. No reports, bearing sensational headlines, are ever issued, but although delegates are sworn to secrecy, minimal leaks, such as noted below, have occurred.

ANNUAL MEETINGS

Bilderbeg delegates, meeting in the year 2002, occupied the entire Westfields Marriott Hotel in Chantilly, Virginia from 31st May to 3rd June: *'Secrecy and Security are the watchwords, and black limousines and helicopters poured into the hotel past a battery of armed guards and FBI agents, paid for – as always – out of the host country's public purse. Previous venues have included Gothenburg in Sweden in May 2001 and the Turnberry Hotel in Ayrshire in May 1988, when Tony Blair was recognised but denied attending. Mr Blair also tried to conceal his attendance at the 1993 Bilderberg conference in Athens. Kenneth Clarke, a member of the group's steering committee and its UK representative who also attended in 1993, and from 1998 to date, has never declared his interest in the House of Commons register. (4)*

The Wesfield Marriot Hotel staff had evidently been instructed, in 2002, to declare to the world that, on the relevant dates, the hotel had been booked for wedding parties. In 2000, the holding of an international croquet tournament, was the camouflage for the block booking by Bilderberg of the Genval Hotel near Brussels (5).

In a free country, any group, say, of scholars or writers, who wish to keep secret, the content of their meetings, might pose no threat to a democratic nation. But when leaders of a democracy, who owe their status to votes cast by fellow citizens, attend regularly, secret political meetings, the situation is entirely different; voters have every right to demand what the politicians, for whom they have voted, are up to.

From scraps of information it seems that the *raison d'etre* of the Bilderbergers matches the Toynbee advocacy of the destruction of national sovereignties and the establishment of this mysterious "New World Order." 'Who', we are bound to ask 'are going to be the supranational bosses of this Brave New World?' Presumably the reply to that question will be: the self-appointed membership of groups similar to Bilderberg, who already, if occasional leaks are to be believed, are able 'behind the scenes' to control important political events, including the choice for election of Presidential and Prime Ministerial candidates. Our confidence in these self appointed prophets was not enhanced by the reason for the resignation of Prince Bernard from Bilderberg in 1976: the Dutch Government revealed that he had accepted a one million US dollar bribe from the Lockheed Corporation (6).

THE TREATY OF ROME

The Bilderbergers also played an important role, 'Behind the Scenes,' in the lead up to the signing, in 1972, of the Treaty of Rome, when the Conservative Premier, Edward Heath, protested that the treaty merely brought the UK into a European Common Market and that it would not destroy national sovereignties – a fine example of *'denying with his lips what he was doing with his hands'*. The series of treaties which followed the deception of Edward Heath have, step by step, removed UK self government; we no longer have a British Fishing industry nor a British Agricultural industry; Brussels Bureaucrats preside over a set-up which exhibits symptoms, typical of corrupt dictatorships.

EU CORRUPTION

In 1999, Bernard Freedman, President of the EU Court of Auditors, in an interview with Stern Magazine, warned of the danger of fraud "bringing down the whole of the EU" (7). A similar warning came from a Brussels official, Paul Buitenen, who, acting as a "Whistle Blower," warned MEPs that the EU Commission hierarchy were blocking attempts to investigate a string of frauds and mismanagement scandals; at that time the EU parliament was about to consider a motion to censure six commissioners for mal-administrations of finances; Buitenen was rewarded for his initiative by temporary suspension from his job. He complained of threats from armed commission security staff (8).

The Court of Auditors, centred in Luxemburgh, have repeatedly refused to approve the EU's £65 billion budget, on account of many irregularities: these included bribery of officials, claims for non existent olive trees, and smuggling excise-free cigarettes – frauds costing taxpayers an estimated £6 billion per annum. New allegations of corruption keep appearing; the EU parliamentarians, themselves, are accused of improperly using their £100,000 office expense allowance, and they voted down a proposal that they must give documentary evidence to justify travel expenses of up to £200,000 (9)...

In view of this tally of fraud and corruption, it is little wonder that by August 2002, the above mentioned Whistle Blower, Paul Buitenen had had enough; despairing of ever being able to reform the EU financial chaos he resigned from his post and returned to Holland. The last straw for him had been the harsh treatment received by the commission's chief accountant, Marta Andreasen, who disclosed that the £62 billion budget was "out of control"; for this disclosure of what seems to have been the true state of affairs, the poor lady was removed from her post and subjected to disciplinary proceedings.

ORWELLIAN NIGHTMARE

The most worrying reflection on this tale of corruption and injustice, is the similarity between what goes on in the EU headquarters and the regimes, so well caricatured by George Orwell, wherein dictators, with their secret police, suppress freedom of speech, and govern by brute force. In a letter to the Daily Telegraph (30th Oct. 2000) Frederick Forsyth, pondering on what might happen with the imposition of an EU legal system, quotes from a 'Tiny Paragraph' from Brussels: *Criticism of the European Union is akin to Blasphemy and could be restricted without violating freedom of speech according to the opinion issued by the Advocate General at the European Court of Justice'* If this really reflects the beliefs of those in charge of the European Union, then, in their eyes, I am clearly guilty of a blasphemy which would elevate the EU to the status of a false God, to be added to my chapter 8 list of modern false Gods and false prophets.

Rodney Atkinson, whose career included six years as a lecturer at the University of Mainz in Germany, acquired deep insight on German political history and ambitions; he draws a parallel between Britain's feeble surrender in 1972 to the rule of Brussels, dominated by Germany, and the 1930s appeasement policy, advocated by a section of the British Establishment, who believed that negotiating with Hitler would secure "Peace in Our Time".

According to Atkinson, the policies advised by Professor Heinrich Hunke, the leading Nazi academic in 1942, are similar to those of the EU – centralised supranational control of trade and prices, and abolition of the right of independent European nations to control their own economies. The Nazis, hoping in 1942 for complete victory, thus planned for a Europe dominated by Germany and Vichy France, which would reap financial favours at the expense of the British. Did Britain and our allies, therefore, fight two European wars in vain? Here are a few examples of EU anomalies:

Since 1897, crofters of Scottish Highlands and Islands have received a modest State subsidy so that they can afford to hire the services of good quality bulls and rams for inseminating their cows and ewes. In 2004 the EU Competition Commissioner ruled that the subsidy was in breach of European "state aid rules" and therefore illegal. At about the same time the Commissioner approved a £2 billion subsidy to the German coal industry. By similar subsidies German collieries have been able to undercut their British competitors. The article in the Sunday Telegraph, bearing this news, also reported that a £2 billion subsidy enabled the French company, Alstom to bid competitively to build the new Cunard liner QM 2.(10)

EU'S REVENGE?

Is it fair to ask if the EU's apparent anti-British discrimination, engineered by France and Germany, has something to do with the defeat, by British arms, of Napoleon's attempt in the 18th century to impose his rule over Europe, and the later defeat by the British and Allies of two attempts by Germany to achieve, in the 20th century, that same European empire which eluded Napoleon? In plain words, are France and Germany, through the EU, taking revenge on the Anglo Saxons for thwarting their plans?

How otherwise can we explain anti-British measures imposed by EU rules such as that which forbids the UK to be self sufficient in liquid milk; Brussels has dictated that at least 20% of our milk must come from across the channel. In his Sunday Telegraph *Notebook* Christopher Booker has given a weekly comprehensive and lucid account of his researches into the iniquities of the Brussels regime.

Since I wrote the last paragraph, Booker has reported how Bowland Dairies in Nelson, an £8 million a year business, employing twenty six employees, has been closed down by the EU Commission's Food and Veterinary Office (FVO) on the grounds that Bowland's product, curd cheese, used mostly by five EU countries is contaminated by antibiotics. The Commission's decision went against our British Foods Standard Agency's (FSA) inspection which declared the product to be perfectly safe. When the dispute was brought to Court, the judge found 'Unreservedly' in favour of the British business. In spite of these findings the Commission went ahead and banned Bowman from further trading (13).

Lunacy is not too strong a word to describe the exposure of the disastrous workings of the Common Fisheries Policy. For instance, in the year 2000, when a steep rise in the price of diesel fuel added to fishery costs, the EU quota system forced Shetland's fishermen to dump back into the sea, tons of dead saleable fish; one named fisherman was forced to dump 1,000 boxes of fish worth £30,000, while French fishermen, in the same waters, were permitted to keep every netted fish, an injustice which, if continued, will end in pollution of the sea and catastrophic reduction of fish stocks. The Norwegians have repudiated this nonsense by staying outside the EU; they have retained control of their territorial waters and so avoided plummeting fish stocks and the destruction of their fishing fleet (11). Their prosperity, along with the prosperity of Switzerland exceeds that of all other European countries; the Swiss also have refused the invitation to join the EU.

Hidden Costs

The cost to the UK of our EU membership is seldom mentioned by our politicians, nor by the BBC, whom some commentators have accused of pro EU bias. EU posters with their circle of stars on a blue background, which occasionally adorn road works give the false impression that the work is done thanks to the generous EU. The truth is that, annually the UK gives far more tax-payers' money to the EU budget than it receives in return; in 2004 our net contribution amounted to £4.3 billion; Tony Blair has agreed to increase these net payments to *over £6 billion* from 2007 until 2013. A research report published by the Bruges Group reckons that these costs of belonging to the EU will amount to an annual payment to Brussels of £873 by every British man, woman and child (12).

If the record of the corrupt rule of the European Union gives a preview of the New World Order, where nations lose their independence and come under the dictatorial rule of a distant centralised bureaucracy, heaven forbid that the World Government activists will have their way. Was it a 'New World Order' that Satan had in mind when, from a high mountain he showed Jesus *'All the Kingdoms of the world and their splendour "all this I will give to you" he said "if you will bow down and worship me" (Matthew,4:8,9.)* The existence of plans, hatched behind the scenes, to bring about a New World Order is not a new phenomenon and some of those plans can indeed be termed Satanic, according to the research of an 18th century Edinburgh Professor, to be discussed in chapter 14.

References

1. Atkinson Rodney, *Europe's Full Circle,* Compuprint, 1966, Newcastle apon Tyne.
2. Ibid pp 65, 66.
3. Ibid.
4. Green Stephen, *Christian Voice,* p2, June 2002, PO Box 739A, Surbiton.
5. Ibid.
6. Dutch Donner Report, 1976.
7. Ambrose Evans-Pritchard *Whistle- Blower admits defeat on EU corruption.* Daily Tel. 29/8/02
8. Ibid.
9. Ibid
10. Sunday Tel. *Scottish Bulls are a red rag to Brussels.* State Aid, 23rd May 2004 .
11. Booker.C. *The dumping of our fishermen,* Sunday Tell. Sept3. 2000. p16.
12. Liberty News No. 14, 2006, Campaign for an Independent Britain
13. Booker C. *A grim legal first killed this firm* Sunday Tel. p16, 10th Dec. 06

CHAPTER 14
THE DEVIL'S SCHEMES

*Put on the full armour of God so that you can take your stand
against the devil's schemes.* (Ephesians, 6: 11)

A MAN OF MANY PARTS

Professor John Robison (1739-1803), son of a Glasgow merchant
and educated at Glasgow Grammar School, after studying Natural
Philosophy, graduated from Glasgow University in 1756. He lived
in the years of the 18th century, termed by historians and
philosophers, as "The Age of Enlightenment" when human reason
sought to take over from traditional custom and religion. After
graduating, Robison took on the job of tutoring a Royal Navy
midshipman, the son of Admiral Knowles; in 1759 young Knowles
embarked with the expeditionary force, commanded by General
Wolfe, which was bound for Canada; evidently it was customary for
the tutor to accompany his pupil, even in war; Robison happened to
be with General Wolfe on the night before the General was killed
during the battle for Quebec.

Later, as private secretary to Admiral Knowles, Robison went to
St. Petersburg and travelled widely in Russia, France and Germany.
On returning from service abroad, he lectured on Chemistry at
Glasgow University, then in 1773 was appointed Professor of
Natural Philosophy at Edinburgh University, in which capacity he
taught Mechanics, Hydro-Dynamics, Astronomy and Optics,
Electricity and Magnetism (1).

He clearly earned the reputation of a man of keen intellect and
wide interests; his knowledge of the science of those days went with
his skill as a musician, so he well deserved election as Secretary of the
Royal Society of Edinburgh. He collaborated with his fellow
scientist, James Watt, and it was Robison who suggested that the
power of steam might be used to drive an engine. After Robison's
death, Watt wrote of him: '*He was a man of the clearest head and
most science of anybody I have known*'. The portrait of Robison by Sir
Henry Raeburn shows a shrewd and kindly face (2).

The above account of the abilities and character of John Robison is given to counter the accusation that any author, pursuing the trail of conspiracies, is simply a conspiracy theory freak, whose beliefs have no substance. Robison was a man of sense and integrity; his book, *Proofs of a Conspiracy against all the Religions and Governments of Europe,* published in Edinburgh and London in 1798, by which time, its author had reached the age of 58, had an immediate impact; the first printing sold out in a few days and was followed by new editions. Robison's findings were fully confirmed in 1799 by the publication of a book, *Memoirs Illustrating the History of Jacobinism* by a French clergyman, Abbe Augustine Barruel. The French churchman and the Scottish Professor had never met and wrote entirely ignorant of each other's beliefs, but both reached the same conclusions on Europe's dark and secret conspiracies.

"Oppressions, Woes and Pains"

Knowledge of the problems facing the European mainland in the closing decades of the 18th century, will help the reader to understand the background of John Robison's book. According to historians, in France, it certainly was *A Time to Weep*: by the 1780s, apart from Britain and Holland, European countries with their multitude of Royal courts were bankrupt, having lost their wealth in the wars of preceding decades. Soaring debt led to higher and higher taxes. In France, Europe's largest country, the Enlightenment's growing shoots of science took place against a background of decadence, corruption and injustice among the leaders of church and nation; an idle and degenerate aristocracy, living in luxury around the gilded court of Louis XIV frittered away their time in indolent dissipation. Aristocratic landowners exempted themselves from the burden of taxation, which was thrust on to the shoulders of their unfortunate peasants. '*The court and the cities drained the countryside dry' (3).*

Bishops and Abbots, having joined the throng of wealthy, idle landowners, neglected their charges for the lusting and dicing of the court; they paid no taxes themselves but exacted cash tributes from their impoverished cures, pastors and rectors, who toiled in the real work of town and country (4).

RISING CRITICISM

A nation, thus riddled with injustice and misery, gave ample cause for the criticism and scorn of a rising middle class and a band of intellectuals and writers led by Jean Jacques Rousseau (1712–78), Voltaire (1694–1778), and Diderot (1713–84); the last-named expressed the wish to see *'the last King, strangled with the entrails of the last priest'* (5).

This was the theatre of simmering discontent observed by our Edinburgh University Professor, John Robison, as he travelled in the European mainland in the years preceding the explosion of the French Revolution. His book *Proofs of a Conspiracy*, is not easy reading; in the following paragraphs, direct quotations from the book are printed in italics.

As a Scottish Free-Mason, enjoying access to the Masonic brotherhood of France and Germany, Robison was surprised to discover a marked difference between the themes discussed at British Lodge meetings and the themes dealt with on the continent:

'..nothing touching religion or government shall ever be spoken of in the (British) *Lodge; meetings were merely a pretext for passing an hour or two in a sort of decent conviviality, or indulging in innocent merriment'.*

In contrast to this easy-going atmosphere, the French lodges had become:

' ...the haunts of many projectors and fanatics, both in science and religion and in politics. They availed themselves of the secrecy and freedom of speech (in the lodges) to broach their particular whim or suspicious documents, which, if published to the world, would expose the authors to ridicule or to censure.'

Robison expressed great alarm at finding in the Masonic lodges of continental Europe, centres of subversion against established religion where:

'..men of licentious principles became more bold and taught doctrines subversive to all our notions of morality and all our confidence in the moral government of the universe'.

DR. WEISHAUPT AND THE ILLUMINATI

Robison's text tends to be repetitive and his ordering of the narrative somewhat difficult to follow. But his evidence is clear that from the Masonic subversives, there sprang another and separate association, the brain-child of a Professor of Cannon Law in the University of Ingolsdadt, Bavaria, Dr. Adam Weishaupt, who had been trained as a Jesuit but thereafter abandoned his Christianity for extreme hostility towards the Jesuits and the Christian faith. With missionary zeal he set out to found and to lead: *A secret union of noble minds.* This secret "union" was named "Illuminati," whose members were pledged to spearhead a world-wide movement with the following objectives, taken not from any formal list, but distilled from Robisons text; italics are again used for words quoted from *Proofs of a Conspiracy.*

1. *'To get possession of riches, power and influence…to accomplish this they want to abolish Christianity…their dissolute manners and a universal profligacy will procure them adherents of all the wicked and enable them to overthrow all the civil governments of Europe.'* Princes and Kings would be removed from the scene as they would hinder the new enlightenment and the making of: *…the human race, without any distinction of nation, condition or profession, one good happy family.* (p 119)
2. *They will seek further conquests and expand their operations to other quarters of the globe til they have reduced mankind to the state of one indistinguishable mass'.* (p 209)
3. Patriotism and loyalty to be seen as narrow minded prejudices, therefore nation states to be abolished and replaced by liberty and equality and the rights of man.
4. They will *'abolish the baneful influence of inherited property and the traditional family; children might be better taken over by the State.*
5. *By enlightening minds and freeing them from superstition and prejudices, men would be made so good that civil governments would be unnecessary; society would go forward peacefully in a state of perfect liberty and equality'.*

Weishaupt had successfully trawled Masonic lodges for recruits or novices to this satanic Society of the Illuminati; the sons of wealthy and influential people were targeted with the promise of new freedoms, especially...*the indulgence of youthful passions and the enjoyment of influence and power.* (End of italics for direct quotations from Robison's book).

SINISTER RITUALS

A chosen novice was subjected to intense, secret grilling over many sessions, in order that his inner mind might be revealed; if not found wanting, he became an 'Illuminatus Minor' who must sign an obligation, binding himself to perpetual silence on his membership and unshakable loyalty and submission to the order. He makes complete surrender of his own will and judgement to his superior and finally, a drawn sword is pointed at his breast as he is asked "will you be obedient to the commands of your superior?"

Robison's account of the progress of the Illuminati is long and detailed; space permits only a brief mention of the apparent success of the order: in Bavaria, members acquired various professorships; monks and Jesuits were thwarted in their work; six members succeeded in penetrating the Royal Court; schools and courts were infiltrated and the revenues of some churches were taken. Infiltration of Masonic lodges by the Illuminati in France brought their influence to bear far and wide in that country.

The Iluminati leaders called themselves the Areopagus and used code names in their correspondence. Weishopt chose 'Sparticus', the famed rebel against Rome. He sought absolute control over some of the degrees of the order and acted with fanaticism typical of a power-drunk dictator. According to him, so good and lofty were the objectives of the Illuminati that any means could be employed for their achievement.

Their subversive tracts began to circulate in Bavaria where members of the Order were encouraged to spy on one another and on those around them; drunkenness and fornication, according to Robison, were rife among the leaders (p135–151). Weishaupt, himself, having seduced his sister-in-law, sought to have the baby which she conceived by him destroyed, or the mother murdered. (p 165)

When these facts came to light in 1783, the Elector of Bavaria banned all secret society meetings, and four professors, suspected of subversion, were summoned before the Council of Enquiry. They admitted membership of the Order and confessed that its objectives included the abolition of Christianity; Weishaupt was banished to Switzerland.

Suppression of the Illuminati in Bavaria did not seem to worry Weishaupt; the Order would spread elsewhere under the guise of a chain of "Reading Societies."

In 1784 one of the 'Areopagus' leaders, code name Philo, defected from the Order and published accounts of some of its activities; he exposed the ambition of Weishaupt to abolish both Christianity and all the state governments of Europe; two years later, in 1786, papers were discovered which revealed the various Orders of the Illuminati and some of their gruesome activities – concocting recipes for procuring abortion, how to copy impressions of official seals, and how to produce a substance which blinds or kills when squirted in the face.

Lists were also discovered of the location of lodges of the Illuminati including eight in England and two in Scotland; another list gives the names, rank or profession of distinguished recruits – many professors, a few counts, several priests and councellors, a duke and a prince and an assortment of military officers, business men and others.

THE FRENCH REVOLUTION

Robison's last, long chapter details the part played by the Illuminati in the events leading up to the storming of the Bastille in 1789 and the ensuing bloody slaughter.

As stated above, throughout France, Masonic lodges had been penetrated by the Illuminati; many of whom, schooled in secrecy, were the leading characters in the terrible events, culminating in an unimaginable scale of slaughter and human degradation; one of these characters, the Duke of Orleans, the 'Illuminated' Grand Master of French Free Masonry sided with the blood-thirsty Parisian mob. Compte de Mirabeau, another member of the Order, an aristocrat turned rebel, wrecked any chance of peaceful reform of the widespread injustices of the French Royalist regime; Louis XIV had in 1798 at last called a meeting of the Three Estates to initiate reforms; but, like Lenin in that later, equally brutal and murderous Russian revolution, Mirabeau, leader of the third estate, refused any path forward but one of terror and violence. Here, in the seething unrest of a decadent and bankrupt France, was the opportunity for the Illuminati to see their fantasies of a New World Order, based on the rule of Reason, come true.

The final chapter of the *Proofs of Conspiracy* is followed by a forty page long *General Reflection* by the author. The gist of these pages, filled with rather long-winded arguments can be summed up in a simple statement to the effect that the conspirators, with their *'Villainous machinations against the peace of the world'* believe that they will not succeed until religion and morality, inseparably connected together, have been extirpated; they (conspirators) teach that the restraints of religion are the *'contrivance of priests and despots in order to get the command of us'* (6).

References

1. The Dictionary of National Biography, the National Library of Scotland.
2. Cockburn. H. *Memorials of my time.* T.N.Foulis, Edinburgh MCMIX.
3. Bryant. A. *Years if Endurance*, Collins London 1942,
4. Ibid p 41.
5. Ibid
6. Robison John, *Proofs of a Conspiracy Against all the Religions and Governments of Europe.* The Americanist Classics Western Islands, Belmont, Massachachusets 02178, 1967

CHAPTER 15
INTELLECTUALS AND PROPHETS

WOLVES IN SHEEP'S CLOTHING

Professor Robison's account of Weishaupt's Illuminati immediately brought to mind the passage from the Gospel of Matthew: '*Watch out for false prophets. They come to you in sheep's clothing but inwardly they are ferocious wolves*'. (Matt. 7: 15).

According to the Jewish tradition, wandering prophets had no fixed abode; they travelled the country, preaching what they believed was the word of God to listeners who, in return, were expected to give them hospitality; they were recognised by their official 'uniform,' a jacket made of sheep's skin worn with the fleece inside and the skin outside. They were expected to honour the convention that while a true prophet must be welcomed and highly honoured, he must not stay with any congregation for more than two days and must not ask for anything but bread; if he asks for money, he is a false prophet; false also, if he settles for a while in a community and does not support himself by working at a trade or craft – he must work to eat. Prophets were still active after the coming of Jesus, and a Christian rule book, the *Didache,* written about 100 AD, in addition to the above rules, also stated: '*Every prophet that teacheth the truth, if he do not what he teacheth, is a false prophet.*' (1)

We know from the Old and New Testament, that, in spite of the convention, the prophesy system was open to abuse by fraudsters who would pretend to be a prophet, by wearing the sheep's skin jacket, and then spent their lives, enjoying prestige and free hospitality. Corrupt and dishonest judges, rulers or princes, as well as false prophets had earned the name of '*Wolf,*' so the disciples of Jesus, to whom He was speaking, would well understand the message (2).

There can have been very few characters on the stage of European history who deserved the epithet, 'Wolf' as much as did Dr. Adam Weishaupt whose life and work, detailed above, in chapter 14 by Professor Robison, gave abundant cause for *A time to Weep*. He, (Weishaupt), a distinguished lecturer on Law at

Ingolstatd University in Bavaria, must have been a powerful, persuasive and forceful personality, convinced that he alone had the power, (after destroying the Christian religion and all civic authorities), to create a New World Order, presided over by 'Noble Minds' of his choosing. Following the discovery of incriminating documents, dealt with in the last chapter, the Illuminati went underground, disguised as 'Reading Societies,' and according to author, Nick Harding, they did not disappear, but continued to spread their influence through Freemasonry which then became divided into Freemasons who were 'Illuminated' or 'Ordinary' (3).

MODERN WOLVES

Did the Illuminati inspire Karl Marx and Lenin whose campaigns, similar to Weishaupt's, preached the abolition of religion, of the private ownership of property, and the creation of a global 'Soviet Paradise' in place of nation states?

Is there not a similarity between the methods of the Illuminati and the twentieth century's proselytising communists of our Universities, who would seek to enrol undergraduates into secret Marxist cells, at a time when their young lives are susceptible to the influence of older men with a message, particularly, if that message included, according to Robison, '*The indulgence of youthful passions and the enjoyment of influence and power*'?

The process is vividly recalled by the Anglo-American author, Michael Straight, in his account of his life as an undergraduate at Trinity College Cambridge in the 1930s (4). He became a bosom pal of John Cornford, the Communist poet, and of John Klugman, a more sinister activist in the university's communist underworld. Looking back on his student days, Straight remembers how these two communists introduced themselves to him and later brought him into the circle which included Guy Burgess and Anthony Blunt. At this time, in a heightened emotional state, because of a break with his girlfriend, Michael Straight found, in his own words, that: '*It was the sense of brotherhood that had opened a new life for me... I'd lived in fear that I'd become incapable of loving. Now I've learned that I'm able to love Communist students, even if I don't love Communism itself. I'm filled with a violent uncontrollable love for them; and extraordinary sense of comradeship. It's unreasonable and inexplicable. It burns within me and I can't express it. I can't get it out.'*

Looking back to these student days with their rapturous evenings, spent in ardent discussion with his new-found friends, as an older and wiser man, he now believes that these sessions were arranged by dedicated communists, simply seeking to swell their ranks. He believes that he was the first student to be recruited by Anthony Blunt.

By methods similar to those described by Michael Straight, Weishaupt, the false prophet, assisted by leaders and mentors whom he had persuaded to join him, seems to have been highly successful in recruiting to the ranks of the Illuminati, novices from the Masonic lodges of France and Bavaria. The recruitment process which involved long hours of interviews, described in the last chapter, in which the novice must swear total obedience to his mentor to whom he must reveal his most innermost thoughts, smacks of brain washing, with a hint of psychoanalysis. The leaders were taking advantage of *'The sense of comradeship'*, experienced by men emerging from adolescence and easily led by unscrupulous 'wolves', expounding violent revolutionary causes which, they teach, will create a Utopia, by getting rid of the restraints imposed by the Christian religion.

TEAM GAMES

There can be a positive aspect in the *'sense of comradeship'*, experienced by young men who cement human relationships by playing energetic team games on our playing fields and who play, not for individual glory, but for the team. Young people, working for worthy causes can foster comradeship; but 'comrade' is the term used by Marxists; 'Brotherhood' or 'Sisterhood' are better terms for the binding together of Christian workers of all ages engaged in worthwhile projects, under the fatherhood of God, in local congregations or farther away.

If Professor Robison's record is correct, in the years leading up to the outbreak of the revolution, the Illuminati, having penetrated many of the French Masonic lodges, played a crucial role in fomenting the violence and slaughter. Without Weishaupt's fanaticism, might the killing have been prevented? All Europe stood aghast at the scale of the violence, but revolutionaries, no doubt influenced by the Illuminati, who for years had been plotting in secret, were convinced that a New World Order was about to dawn; the destruction of ecclesiastical buildings throughout France and the systematic, brutal murder of their occupants surely speaks of nation-wide planning and preparation. It seems probable that Weishaupt, convinced of the truth of his message and of his own abilities, responded to the refusal of his Jesuit brethren to join the Illuminati, with hatred towards them and abhorrence of all Christianity.

BIBLICAL INTELLECTUALS

In his fascinating account of the lives of intellectuals, Paul Johnson suggests that they play a role, in some ways similar to biblical prophets; this suggestion, can be applied to modern Intellectuals as well as to those of the Enlightenment whose influence can still be felt today (5).. My dictionary's definition of *Intellectual* includes '...*well endowed with intellect*', and ' *person of superior intellect or enlightenment*'; is it fair to conclude that the membership of the Bilderberg Group, featured in chapter 13, can be matched with the Illuminati of the18th century? Although we have no modern investigator like Professor Robison, we can safely conclude that the majority of members of both organisations can be classed as intellectuals, and in spite of the veil of secrecy we can also guess that violence, bizarre rituals of Illuminati novices, and campaigns against Christianity are not on the Bilderburg agenda.

But the motives, membership and make up of the Bilderberg Group do give the following disturbing similarity to the eighteenth century Illuminati;

a) Total secrecy of the identity of members and of proceedings.

b) Members are chosen from intellectuals, including influential leaders in politics, industry, banking and media.

c) The abolition of independent nation states which will be replaced by a New World Order (for which purpose the EU is a first step).

d) Working 'behind the scenes' to influence the policies of national governments.

The Noble savage

One of the 18th century intellectuals whose influence, according to Paul Johnson, can still be felt in modern times, was Jean Jacques Rousseau, born in Geneva, but spending most of his life in France. He first became famous when, aged 37, in 1749 he won an essay competition, offered by the Dijon Academy of Letters. He treated the subject – *The Effect of Progress and Civilisation on Human Morals* – in a manner, different from all the other entrants, by arguing that progress and civilisation robbed man of his freedom and nobility; in later books he expressed his views in vivid, impassioned prose, condemning the artificiality of life in the growing cities of those days, particularly, he denounced rivalry in commerce and accumulation of property; against these he championed the virtues of unsophisticated nature. In 1762, his masterpiece *Contrat Social* tried to solve the problem of why man who was born free, was '...*everywhere in chains*'. He died in 1778, eleven years before the French Revolution, but it was Rousseau's words, 'Liberty, Equality and Fraternity' which became the Revolution's slogan.

Was Rousseau Green?

Was he, as suggested by Paul Johnson, the forerunner of today's Green movement?

It is very doubtful, in my opinion, if that movement owes its existence to the life and work of Rousseau; his beliefs certainly had many features of which the Greens would approve, but his name does not appear at all in the literature of ecologists nor of the Soil Association, an organisation which can claim to have been in the forefront of what is now called the Green movement. Twentieth century scientists such as Sir Albert Howard, Sir Robert McCarrison, and the American writer, Weston Price, rather than an eighteenth century intellectual, paved the way for our understanding of the laws of nature and the importance of obeying those laws in our management of the earth's riches.

It may be that Rousseau's ideas on education partly influenced the officials who, in recent years, introduced 'liberal' teaching methods to the classrooms of British State-run schools which, to many parents, seemed daft, and which seriously impaired the ability of children to express themselves in writing. Please believe that the following conversation, between a Scottish University tutor and an undergraduate, reported in a Broadsheet newspaper, probably in the early 1970s, really did take place (I have lost the reference and the quotation is from memory).

Tutor: *'Your ideas in this essay are not bad, but you must not write a complete sentence without a verb'.* Student: *'But what is a verb?'*

Rousseau was a good example of one of the qualities of a false prophet – *if he do not what he teacheth.* He railed against the sophistication of cities and criticised mothers in their up-bringing of infants, but all the five babies which he fathered by his mistress, Therese le Vasseur, were not reared at their mother's breast, according to *'what he teacheth',* but, immediately after birth, were handed over to a foundling hospital where they were unlikely to survive.

Perhaps we should not be too critical about Rousseau. His mother died at his birth and he grew up in a chaotic parental background; in spite of having no formal education, he became a brilliant writer and skilled musician. Unfortunately, apart from his mistress, Therese, he was incapable of making lasting human relationships, and quarrelled with most of the people he met; he would have been diagnosed today as a having a 'Psychopathic Personality.' His life fitted an other dictionary definition of the term, intellectual – *'Often used to suggest doubt as to practical sagacity.'* But as Rousseau grew older his mind deteriorated beyond a low level of 'practical sagacity' into outright insanity: *'Seeking shelter in a hospital he eventually died, insane, in a cottage at Ermenonville, July 2, 1778, from a sudden attack of thrombosis, which long aroused suspicion of suicide. (6)*

As a postscript to this chapter, I feel that I must report how, repeatedly, when I have become stuck in my somewhat muddled attempt to write this book, as if in answer to my prayers, a document or a lost file has turned up to solve the problem. As I grappled with paragraphs on Bilderbergers, Masons, and Illuminati, Lo and Behold! there appeared this book, *Secret Societies,* by Nick Harding. – a Christmas present to me from my son.

According to Nick Harding, since the dawn of human history, the males of the homo sapiens species have felt the need to form secret societies; some 39 such societies, reviewed in his book may be, he writes, an expression of immaturity, a return to the days when children loved to make their own little dens.

GNOSTICS

The Gnostics, established in the first six centuries of the Christian era, one of the earliest known Secret Societies, having blended their Christianity with Greek and Oriental philosophies, saw themselves as an intellectual elite whose members sought knowledge of a mystical supreme divine power; this knowledge could be acquired if the mind of the initiate was purified, step by step, either by frenzy and excitement or by fasting and meditation, processes which would raise him spiritually far above the mortals stranded down in the evil material world. The few who made it to the desired state of 'purification' by enduring strange initiation rituals could then use secret passwords or hand shakes – a pattern of behaviour adopted by other secret societies (7).

Was I wrong, as I browsed through the book, *Secret Societies,* by Nick Harding to mutter a couplet, often quoted by my father: *'Far beyond the human sight / of those whose heads are screwed on right'* ?

I should not be too dismissive of these mental processes; my own experience does confirm the work of some scientists who conclude that states of altered consciousness can be induced by serious accidents, fatigue, fear, anger or excitement. These states of mind can also be used not only for initiates of secret societies, but as tools of unscrupulous operators who force victims to accept ideas which he or she would normally reject (8). This subject will be pursued in chapter 16.

REFERENCES

1. Barclay, W. *The Gospel of Matthew pp 281-282,* The Saint Andrew Press, Edinbugh, 1977
2. Ibid.
3. Harding Nick, *Secret Societies, p87,* Pocket Essentials, 2005, Harpenden Herts.
4. Straight Michael, *After Long Silence,* Collins 1983.
5. Johnson Paul, *Intellectuals,* Weidenfield and Nicholson, London 1988
6. *Chambers Biographical Dictionary* W&R Chambers Ltd, Edinburgh 1978.
7. Harding Nick, *Secret Societies,* p67, Pocket Essentials, 2005, Harpenden, Herts.
8. Sargant William, *Battle for the Mind* Pan Books, London, 1966.

CHAPTER 16
THE USES OF ADVERSITY 1

*'Sweet are the uses of adversity which like the toad, ugly
and venomous, wears yet a precious jewel in his head'.*
Shakespeare's *As you like it,* .Act 2.

In the 1970s I had to speak frequently at meetings of the McCarrison Society, and to give occasional lectures, on rural practice, to trainees at the general practice departments of Edinburgh or Glasgow University. As a hopeless extempore speaker, I had to find time to write out lectures, and to use a tape recorder for monitoring their quality. During working hours, often in the car while doing home visits, I would find myself trying, urgently, to compose in my head, a lecture soon to be delivered. Occasionally, if I had been out in the middle of the night on an emergency call, when fighting mental fatigue on the next day, it was extraordinary to experience, in the midst of exhaustion, occasional moments of exceptional mental clarity, which solved, in a flash, how I should deal with a lecture's difficult passage. Do these moments of inspiration occur when the creative, unconscious part of the brain is enabled to work more easily because the cells of the brain which control waking consciousness, are too tired, from loss of sleep, to interfere?

Before recounting another, more dramatic instance, of the way in which consciousness can be altered by the adversity of fatigue, trauma or accident, I must apologise for detailing below, my experiences as a hospital patient; such accounts are apt to be boring but there was no other way of dealing with '*The Uses of Adversity*':

'After all those years of the joys of skiing on the rock-strewn slopes of Scotland, that it should happen in this lovely, open, sunlit snowfield was inexplicable. Anger, humiliation, shame, surge up with the sudden blinding pain; with my face pressed against the snow, I want to cry, far more from mental than from physical agony; there is no doubt that the right tibia has gone; I can feel the hard edge of the shattered shaft and see the gross deformity of the lower leg.'

The ingredients were all here for the family holiday we had planned, saved for, and talked about: the magnificence of the High Tyrol in April; firm, easy spring snow.

On this last 'Schuss' home, on the second day of our fortnight, the cool glass of beer and friendly talk around the little tables in the sunshine were almost in sight. Then comes this ghastly explosion of snow, skis and ski sticks. In those first dreadful seconds, consciousness is momentarily blurred; thoughts and images flash to and fro – weeks and weeks in full length plaster – practice partner, Hamish, due his holiday soon after my return – can you do home visits in a full length plaster with crutches? — or confinements? The decent German family who gathered round seemed highly amused when I said that I was a doctor. My own laughter was just a little forced. Bone crepitus, (the crackling caused by the rubbing together of the ends of fractured bones), is not exactly a hilarious sensation'... a mountain rescue squad arrived in good time.

'Whoever thought of the inflatable splint deserves mankind's undying thanks. As the pressure of the inflating air increases, there comes a point when pain relief is instant, and the journey on the stretcher sledge is much less painful than it otherwise would be. The village GP, a man of few words, quickly x-rayed my leg in his well-equipped little surgery ...My poor wife, Sonia, summoned from her ski class, had hardly time to shove a few things into a suitcase, before I was speeding to a hospital in Innsbruck, some 100 kilometres away. Within about fifteen minutes of admission I slipped into the blissful oblivion of intravenous anaesthesia.

So here I am, with my right leg in traction, tended by charming nuns who, with their assistants, staff this hospital. There is much laughter at my pathetic attempts to master the German tongue...In the sudden forced helplessness and isolation, my hectic chasing of the clock as a rural GP seems a misty dream. There are hours to lie and think, as the sound of the church bells of Innsbruck come lazily over the roof tops...

...An assistant nurse has just come in to fix a small palm leaf to the crucifix on the wall. Here, in Austria, bells are ringing out in anticipation of the joy and renewal of Easter'.(1)

A long metal pin had been driven through my right heel bone, to be connected to the bracket, tied to the cord, pulley and weight, hanging over the raised splint at the foot of the bed – an efficient contraption for maintaining steady traction to keep the broken shaft of the shin bone in place. The crucifix, with its palm leaf, reminded me that when His bones were pierced, no anaesthetic was given to Jesus. For the celebration of Easter a choir of Nuns processed along the hospital corridor, singing Easter hymns; their harmony can truly be described as heavenly, wonderful; was this part of adversity's 'precious jewel'? The choir certainly helped to lighten the mood of the awful remorse I had suffered for letting down my wife and family.

It is difficult to define and explain my emotions, as I wanted to weep in the ambulance run to the hospital, and knew that there was no one to blame for what had happened, but myself. After ski school I may have been going too fast on the run back to base; I did not want to collide with the skier ahead of me and had taken my eyes off the piste surface which was rutted and hard; worst of all, I had not properly checked my ski safety release catch, designed to prevent the sudden torsion imposed on leg bones when a ski edge gets caught and the skier twists as he falls heavily.

Does serious trauma, the breaking of bones, so alter our spirit that we come nearer to God, as suggested in the Hymn 'Nearer, my god to thee'? There was no doubt that through pain and bitter remorse, my consciousness had entered unknown territory; sorrow and remorse dominated my thoughts, but so did a strange certainty of Divine presence which is very difficult to describe – a state of mind expressed years ago by our foot soldiers in rather unpoetic language, as the enemy mortar bombs and artillery shells fall perilously close: 'Ye'll no find an atheist in a slit trench'.

When I arrived, with my X-Ray plates, at the Innsbruck hospital, the Sanatorium Kreuchzwester, chosen by the village GP, it was impressive to realise that the surgeon, Dr. Offer, who had been informed, by phone, of my coming, was waiting for me with his anaesthetist. It is perhaps unjust to compare this efficiency with what can happen in our NHS hospital outpatient departments. Coping with skiing injuries is repeatedly rehearsed by medical professionals working near a popular skiing resort. Another contrast to the NHS is that all the services which I had used – the Mountain Rescue, the GP with his X-ray, the ambulance, and the hospital had been paid for, not by the tax payers of Austria, but by the insurance company to which I had subscribed.

The contrast in hospital care was highlighted, when some six weeks after my return home, an appointment had been made with my nearest NHS Orthopaedic Department, so that the full length plaster could be changed; when I arrived at the clinic the consultant, who did not seem very interested, as he sat back in his chair, greeted me thus: *'It's a pity you've come today, because the plaster technician is on holiday.'*

I was handed over to the tender mercies of a junior doctor whom I had to help as he was not very good at using plaster shears.

The fundamental flaw in our state-run medical service rests in the triumphant, oft repeated slogan, "Free at the time of use"; this slogan defies reality; medical services are not free, they have to be paid for. In all advanced nations, except the UK, as far as I know, systems of state and private insurance enable the patient to pay the cost of both GP and hospital care "at the time of use"; having paid for care, the patient, through these insurance schemes, can retrieve all or most of the cost. Low income patients, unable to afford insurance or fees are not denied full medical care, payments for meals have to be made to hospitals. The virtue of this regime is that costs are paid for "at the time of use" and so income is generated according to the value of every service. The weakness of our state-run NHS is that medical care is paid for, out of general taxation, so that allocation of cash has to meet the demands of other public services – local authorities, armed forces, schools, transport, contribution to the EU and many more; there is never enough cash.

POLITICAL IDEOLOGY

In one of the books, *The Gulag Archipelago*, which my wife had packed for my journey to the Innsbruck hospital, Alexander Solzhenitsyn, writing from his experience of the terrible Soviet system, states *'Ideology is what gives evil-doing the necessary steadfastness and determination… thanks to ideology the twentieth century was fated to experience evil- doing on a scale calculated in millions. This cannot be denied or passed over'.* Thanks to Soviet ideology, *'the communist police apparatus which would eventually grind up some sixty million victims was set up by Trotsky, and Dzerzhinsky'*; this death toll did not include the millions of peasants who perished under the rule of the Soviets.(2) The Fascist ideology of Hitler's Germany adds to the 20th century's scale of death and misery, *'calculated in millions'.*

The faults of the NHS cannot, of course, be bracketed with evil-doing on Solzhenitsyn's scale but, to quote from James Bartholomew's account of how the NHS was founded in 1948: *'The driving ambition does not come from the failings of the existing healthcare system It comes from a political ideology'* (3).

After the 1945 election triumph of the Labour Party, the new prime minister, Clement Attlee, was so impressed with the reputation of Aneurin Bevan whose ideology and thinking were ' rooted in Marxism,'(4) that he put him in charge of health and housing.

In reviewing the part played by Bevan in creating the NHS, his family background in a Monmouthshire mining village should not be forgotten. One of a family of ten, whose father would depart for the pit every morning at 5.30 am., young Aneurin left school, aged fourteen, to follow his father and work as a miner; from childhood, a rebel and revolutionary, as he grew up, he soon made his mark in his union lodge as a brilliant debater; *'He had guile, charm, a terrific memory and great debating skills. Many members of his own party wanted him to fall flat on his face but he did not.'* (5) Is an ideology *'rooted in Marxism'* inevitable, when miners, at the coalface, compare their lot with workers in other occupations?

Opinions differ on the state of medical care before 1948; most doctors, old enough to have experienced pre-NHS medicine, would, I believe, agree that before 1948 there were no significant failings in UK hospitals, nor was there any crying out for reform. But in an article on how the NHS should, in 2007 "Dig itself out of the financial hole in which it found itself wallowing," a writer states in the BMJ that any move towards privatisation "...will be catastrophic for the public health and return to the gross inequities which were in place before 1948." (6) It would be useful to have references identifying these 'gross inequities'.

CHARITY HOSPITALS

From the eighteenth century, the building, nation-wide, of Voluntary (i.e. Charitable) Hospitals rapidly expanded, thanks to the generosity of groups or individuals, motivated by Christian giving. More than four hundred were built between 1850 and 1906. In his speech at the ceremony to mark his retiring in 1902, the Physician-Superintendent of the Gartnavel Royal Asylum, Glasgow, stated: '...*Now, the condition of the insane poor is a triumph of practical Christianity. They are housed, fed and surrounded with comforts and elegancies as they never could have been but for their insanity. The feeling of the public towards insanity has also changed greatly. It is no longer regarded a doom and a horror, but as a disease involving no more reproach or blame as other diseases.*'(7)

Many of today's patients do not know that, before the coming of the NHS, consultants, who worked and taught in the voluntary teaching hospitals, did not receive remuneration; their income would come from private patients, referred to them by GPs whom they had taught as students. Resident junior teaching hospital doctors received no salary during their stay in hospital; they regarded the job as valuable experience and received only board and lodging.

Pre-NHS hospitals, established by charitable giving, earned the loyalty of the communities which they served. Some beds were sustained by endowments, or legacies, and some hospitals used payment schemes whereby contributors who gave regular annual payments earned free treatment when the need arose. Lady Almoners negotiated fees with those able to pay. Out patient departments were open to all comers.

WARD SISTERS

The 'back bone' of patient care in hospital wards lay in the hands of the disciplined nursing teams led by the ward sisters, presided over by the hospital matrons. The word 'discipline' is used because as in any team effort, the quality of service and the morale of the team depends on the leader; I cannot remember when or why the disastrous down-grading of the status of ward sisters occurred, but I believe that 'disaster' is the correct word. (The use of the title, 'sister' harks back to the ladies who devoted their lives to caring for the sick in early Catholic Christian establishments; do today's bureaucrats want to erase all traces of Christian origins?).

Some years ago, when visiting a patient who happened to be in a ward of Edinburgh Royal Infirmary in which I had worked as a student, it was sad to observe the untidiness of the entrance area which I remembered as a polished place, spic and span, where students, who wished to enter the ward, would respectfully tap on the door of sister's office to ask permission.

Accounts of filthy toilets and unclean wards are too numerous and serious to write off as an example of the nostalgic ramblings of the aged; there is widespread agreement that this failure of discipline brings the ravages of the MRSA and other infections. The transfer of ward cleaning from hospital employees to outside contractors may have contributed to falling standards. UK hospitals have by far the highest percentage of contamination by the MRSA germ than any other country in northern Europe.

Here are two examples of an absence of discipline in hospitals: a) When a consultant physician arrived to take his Monday afternoon clinic he was told that the clinic had been cancelled. Why? The staff had decided that they would not work on a public holiday; alright! But would it not have been wise, decent, civilised to discuss the matter with the consultant? b) A consultant surgeon advised that an ambulance should be used for the fifty mile journey from hospital to the home of a patient, recovering from an operation which required that his leg should be elevated on the long journey. The ambulance crew at first refused to go, because the patient could (just) walk.

The demoting of ward sisters, seems to have been followed by a huge increase in the number of hospital managers, administrators and support staff; one study recorded that for every ten NHS hospital nurses, there were eight managers and support staff, whereas for every ten nurses, in a private hospital, the ratio of managers and support staff per ten nurses was 1.8 (8). With every reorganisation of the NHS the numbers of administrators increased.

British medicine, before the NHS, seen as a world leader, attracted students from many countries. To quote again from James Bartholomew:

'Hospitals and beds were plentiful. Britain was a leader in a wide variety of specialities. A great richness of hospitals existed in 1948. They were world leaders and world teachers'. (9)

In the Perth Royal Infirmary, in which I worked in 1946/47, the consultant Radiologist acted as the Administrative Medical Officer who was assisted by a competent secretary; as far as I know, there were no other managers.

Here is a final comment on NHS hospitals from a medical consultant: '...*we now have in one of the hospitals in which I work no fewer than nine medical audit facilitators, two audit supervisors and one director of medical audit. Their salaries and other costs must be at least £500,000 per annum. One cannot help but wonder what audit facilitators did before they were employed as such.*' (10)

SKIER'S
(ANAESTHETIC!)
DREAM

SANATORIUM
KREUCHZNESTER
INNSBRUCK
EASTER 1976

Skier's (Anaesthetic!) Dream

REFERENCES

1. Yellowlees W. Text in *Italics* taken from *Personal View,* BMJ p 173, 17th July 1976
2. Solzhenitzyn A. *The Mortal Danger,* The Bodley Head, London 1980.
3. Bartholomew James *The Welfare State We're In,* Methuen Publishing Ltd, London 2004.
4. Ibid, p 89.
5. Ibid p 89.
6. Pollock A. *One Year to save the NHS.* BMJ, vol .334, p 180, 27th Jan. 07.
7. Amicitiae Memor. Printed in Glasgow for private circuation, 1904. Account of Proceedings of 31st Jan. and 9th Oct 1902 in honour of David Yellowlees MD LLD, and Mrs Yellowlees.
8. Barthomew James *The Welfare State We're in,* Methuen Publishing Ltd, London 2004
9. Ibid. p 102.
10. Dalrymple Theodore, *Doctors, Patients and other Nuisances,* The Spectator, p 8, 21 May 2004.

CHAPTER 17
WEEP FOR THE NHS

An essential hallmark, of any civilised nation, is a medical care system which will not deny to any patient, however impoverished, access to good hospital or GP care. Before the coming of the NHS this aim was usually upheld by general practitioners who gave free consultations to those whom they knew were unable to pay. In the voluntary hospitals, as stated in the last chapter, free care was available. Friendly Societies gave to their members, protection from life's risks including sickness (1).

The reluctance of any advanced country to follow Britain's example, of a "free", state-run, medical service, is an interesting indication of the image, seen by other nations, of the British NHS. Is their reluctance in this matter, due to their belief that a centralised system, financed out of general taxation, run by an army of administrators and managers, will always run out of cash? Do they perceive that demands on national expenses, state education, the state's armed forces, the state's pensions and so on, will, inevitably, penalise medical services which are burdened by excessive administrative costs?

Countries which have not gone down the road of nationalised medicine, have decided that the only way to finance medical care is to pay for every service at the time of use. Such a system ensures that GPs and hospitals generate income according to patient demands. Various insurance schemes, some run by trades unions, will reimburse all or most of the fees paid to GPs or hospitals; premiums paid for sickness insurance should, in fairness, be free of income tax. How does this system work for poverty stricken patients? In France, various categories of low income groups are not required to pay full fees; the system there has not given rise to suffering among the poor.

The sad performance of some of our NHS hospitals is often revealed by accounts of clinical episodes given by ex-patients. Such accounts vary enormously; there are horror stories of long waiting lists, of operations cancelled at the last minute, of sometimes fatal hospital infections, of poor nursing, especially for elderly patients, of filthy toilets, (already mentioned in my last chapter), of lost hospital records and of poor communications between consultants, patients and GPs.

Here is one anecdote about a frail 88 year old friend who lived alone, his wife having died; there were no children. He was admitted to hospital, following an accident which fractured his breast bone; although still severely incapacitated, after a few days in hospital, he was told, somewhat brusquely that it was time for him to go home, with the words: "This is not an hotel." He clearly would have had great difficulty in looking after himself, on his own; the hospital staff evidently did not know, nor did they seem to care about his home situation.

The provincial hospital in which I worked in 1941/42, years before the coming of the NHS, used a small Convalescent Home, near the hospital, which cared for patients, such as my friend, who did not need further hospital treatment, but were judged to be not yet fit to go home.

Of course, the quality of care in the NHS is not all negative; horror stories are frequently countered by tales of excellent care, told by grateful ex-patients. But there is no doubt that in many hospitals, *Caritas* (loving care, as defined by St.Paul (2)) so prominent in the nineteenth and early twentieth century's hospitals, is sadly lacking. Medical scientists disapprove of individual anecdotes, such as the one I have given above, as evidence of standards of medical or surgical care, so the data, comparing the performance of UK hospitals with what happens in the wards of other advanced nations, collected and published by James Bartholomew (3), are of great importance. His graphs, made from impeccable sources, showing the performance of our UK hospitals, give a devastating indictment of a centralised, "free", state-run medical service. The data given under the following four headings are taken from James 's book *The Welfare State We're In.*

HOW MANY HOSPITAL BEDS?

According to Department of Health figures, from 1990/1 to 2000/1, more than 50,000 hospital beds became unavailable in England.

Data from OECD and WHO, giving the *number of beds per one thousand of population*, tell us that Japan has over 16 beds, Australia and France have approximately 8, the UK, 4.

HOW MANY CT SCANNERS?

CT scanners are very valuable tools for diagnostic purposes. Here are figures from OECD health data, for 1999 or earlier, giving the number of scanners per one million of population: Japan has over 80, Australia, Switzerland, Germany and France, have 10 or over, the UK has 5.

HOW MANY PATIENTS HAVE TO WAIT OVER FOUR MONTHS FOR SURGERY?

The following figures give the percentage of patients, hospitalised, or needing elective surgery, who have waited, in various countries, for four months or more:

USA 1%, Australia 17%, New Zealand 22%, UK 33%.

HOW MANY PATIENTS DIE FROM MRSA?

The figure, often quoted, of 5000 deaths in the UK hospitals from MRSA, is unreliable and probably a gross understatement. Hospital doctors, for obvious reasons, may avoid putting *MRSA infection* on the death certificate of a patient, admitted on account of some other disease .In a study by the *European Antimicrobial Resistance Surveillance System,* samples of bacteria were taken from the hospitals of several countries around Europe. The idea was to discover, in each country, the percentage of hospitals, harbouring the bacterium *Staphylococcus Aureus* which, because it was resistant to the antibiotic, Methicillin, could cause fatal infections; *Staph. Aureus* is a germ which survives in dust, human skin or clothing and can be carried in human nasal passages. To quote from James Bartholomew on the European study's findings of the presence of this bug in hospitals: *'The results showed a clear north-south divide. Countries surrounding the Mediterranean had a much higher incidence of it. However there was one break in the pattern. In Britain, the proportion of MRSA was 46.1 per cent – above the levels even of the Mediterranean countries and far higher than that of the northern countries'.* This study (published in 2002) found no Resistant Staph. Aureus presence at all in Netherland's hospitals, only one per cent in Sweden's and Finland's; the UK's score was 46% – approaching half of our hospitals.

The simple solution for this awful problem is the discipline of maintaining clean floors, furnishings, toilets, and strict hand washing by staff, and why not sterile gowns for visitors? The root of the problem is probably the employment, to cut costs, of outside cleaners who resent control by the senior nurses.

Recently another germ, *clostridium difficile,* has emerged in NHS hospitals as the cause of severe diarrhoea and sickness, resulting from a well known, disturbing side effect of antibiotics – the elimination, in the colon, of friendly bacteria, which live naturally there, where they keep the balance between friendly and hostile bacteria; the spread of *clostridium[1] difficile* infection can, of course, be transmitted, from patient to patient, where hygiene is poor.

Pre NHS, apart from local authority hospitals, all others, often founded originally by individual Christian philanthropists, supported by fund-raising campaigns, sought to be self supporting; a senior doctor, known as the 'Physician Superintendent,' looked after administration. In 1902 at a dinner to mark his retirement after twenty-seven years at Gartnavel Mental Hospital, Glasgow, the Physician Superintendent, declared in his speech, *'God gave me his best blessing in giving me as my life's work, work that was entirely congenial.'* After giving impressive figures for patients discharged, completely recovered, he was able to report that a debt amounting to £11,000 in 1874, had been paid off and a fund amounting to £34,000 now accumulated (4). The speech, quoted above, echoes my chapter one's report of the words of Arthur Stoddard, laced with biblical language, expressing gratitude to the *'Giver of all good,'* spoken at the opening of a public hall and reading room in the

---

[1] *Clostridium* is the name given to a group of anaerobic bacteria

village of Eldersli.e. in 1881. Thus, a physician and an industrialist, over a hundred years ago, did not hesitate to express their belief in and gratitude for a living God.

In 1948 all voluntary hospitals were embraced in the Godless grip of the state which seized all hospital assets via regional hospital boards – an expropriation of property, akin to Henry VIII's seizure of monasteries! (5) Soon, as regional hospital boards, gave way to Area Health Boards, hospital staffs were subjected to seemingly endless reorganisations.

NHS AND THE GP IMPROVEMENTS

Before July 1948 the consulting room of most GPs was on the ground floor of the doctor's family house. Often, facilities were inadequate for diagnostic purposes and space too limited for secretarial or nursing help, or for the storing of records. In most practices, run by a married GP, his wife acted as receptionist and (before the invention of phone-answer machines) as telephonist; housemaids or daily cleaners would answer the phone in the wife's absence.

The NHS encouraged much needed improvement; Health Centres became possible by the grouping of GPs and the employment of full-time staff. However, in the 1950s, many family doctors were sorely pressed, as the abolition of fees brought a surge of demand. Owing to the new system of payments, the harder the GP worked and the better his service, the worse was his or her pay.

Anomalies in remuneration affected doctors in areas where crowds of tourists increased demands in the holiday months. The tourist, seeking NHS care, signed a "temporary resident" form which allowed him "free" medical care; but the rate of payment to the doctor, when the forms were submitted to the paying authority, as far as I remember, in those days about £1.60, was uniform; i.e. payment to the doctor for one consultation was no different from the fee awarded for several visits to the patient's caravan or guest house, nor was any further payment made if, as sometimes happened, the tourist had to be admitted to the cottage hospital. (The present day temporary resident fee is £25) Here is an example: a middle aged man who, in the days before the creation of hospital coronary care units, while on holiday, suffered a classical, severe episode of coronary thrombosis; he was admitted to the Aberfeldy Cottage Hospital where he remained for about three weeks and made a good recovery; all for £1.60! (As if in a jewellers shop, a diamond tiara was sold at the same price as a cheap ring).

Those who drew up the pay structure for general practice did not seem to know about cottage hospital out patient departments where we stitched wounds, X-rayed for minor fractures, thus often saving patients the round trip of about 60 miles to the nearest larger hospital, all for no pay!

GP Revolt

Examples abound of how the "free" service often encouraged unthinking patients to take advantage of overworked GPs: an elderly lady lived about seven miles away and, in the days of far less car ownership than now, required regular visits for her various infirmities; when I visited her cottage on the day of the routine visit, the door was locked. She had gone into Aberfeldy for an appointment with the hairdresser!

At about 9.30 pm, on a winter evening, when I was at my desk in the consulting room, then situated in the middle of the village, trying to do some paper work, there came a ring at the front door bell "*I saw that your light was on, doctor*" said the patient, "*and I thought you wouldn't mind renewing my prescription*".

I have described elsewhere, the *urgent* demand for a visit on a Sunday morning, from a patient, living about six miles away; he showed every sign of health and comfort as he lay in bed: his complaint? He was feeling tired. In the first decade of the "free" access to doctors, so harsh were conditions in general practice and so low the morale of GPs that many young doctors fled to other lands. The records of actual numbers may be filed somewhere, I can immediately name five of my contemporaries of whom two went to Canada, two to Australia and one to New Zealand. All were keen on their profession and gifted academically.

Things came to a head in the 1960s when, in a scheme, organised by the BMA, GPs en masse signed undated letters of resignation from the Health Service, to be delivered to the Health

Minister unless conditions improved. A new GP charter, which transformed standards and rewards in practice, emerged from this controversy.

Improvement of premises and employment of nursing or secretarial staff could now be afforded. The foundation of the College of GPs, soon to be recognised as the Royal College, was a further step raising standards of care by family doctors.

THE BEVERIDGE REPORT

I cannot leave this criticism of a centralised system of medical care, run by the state, employing a multitude of bureaucrats, without referring to the Orwellian use of the word "Health". The NHS was conceived in Sir William Beveridge's Report published in 1942 which was hailed with enthusiasm; compulsory National Insurance, in post war Britain, would bring universal social security and would defeat the 'five giants' who threatened the welfare of our nation: *want, ignorance, diseases, squalor and idleness'*. (5) Optimists believed that if everyone had access to free medical care, the giant, *disease,* would be defeated and the nation's health would improve to such an extent that soon the costs of ill health would significantly fall.

This view was profoundly wrong. "Free" medical care does not create health. Advances in medical and surgical treatment during the second half of the twentieth century have been impressive; the success of new surgical techniques, joint replacement, eye cataract operations, coronary by-pass techniques are matched by pharmaceutical discoveries giving 'wonder drugs' bringing some relief to those who suffer from various physical or mental ailments. But these improvements do not create health; they are repair jobs for damage, which, in the opinion of many distinguished scientists is caused by our dreadful dietary habits.

The problem rests in the attitude which permeates our medical schools, encouraged by powerful pharmaceutical firms to believe that the cure for our widespread degenerative diseases will come from new drugs. Those who teach medical students seem to be unaware of the way to health, published by pioneers in human nutrition and ecology during the 20th century – Sir Robert McCarrison, Lord Boyd Orr, the American dentist Weston Price, Francis M Pottenger

MD , the botanist Sir Albert Howard, the agriculturist Lady Eve Balfour, American biochemist Professor Ross Hume Hall, physicians TL Cleave, Denis Burkit and many others.

THE HEALTH EDUCATION COUNCIL

In 1976, the late Dr. Kenneth Barlow and I, as members of the McCarrison Society, were granted an interview with the late Sir George Godber a former Chief Medical Officer, and then Chairman of the Health Education Council. We put to him McCarrison's compelling conclusions, published in 1936, after a lifetime of nutrition research, that the greatest single factor in creating health rested, not in a state-run Health Service, but in sound nutrition, the consumption of *'The unsophisticated foods of nature'* rather than processed, refined products, laced with dyes, sweeteners and other artificial additives (6). We suggested that one measure by the Health Education Council could be a good start, a campaign to encourage the consumption of bread made from whole wheat flour rather than from refined, constipating white flour. We also put to him, Cleave's evidence on the role of refined sugar as the cause of coronary heart disease (7).

Sir George thanked us for coming, but was clearly unimpressed with our views; a few days after the interview I received a letter from a member of his staff, stating *'we will keep the points you made at our meeting carefully in mind...I have asked Van den Berghs and Jurgens Ltd. to send you details of their activities in this area'*. The packet of documents duly arrived from the makers of Flora margarine; readers may recall that chapter 6 of this book gives an account of Van den Bergh's relationships with senior doctors. Here is *A Time to Weep* over official 'Health' departments, who appear to be in the pockets of powerful, wealthy food processors; thus, Government health advisers dismiss advice, based on sound research, and hearken to firms whose motives are simply to boost the sales of their product. So, the nation's slices of constipating white bread, will no doubt continue to be spread with fabricated polyunsaturated margarine instead of nature's butter.

In that same year, 1976, another attempt failed to enlighten doctors, this time GPs. In an interview with the chairman of the education committee of the Royal College of General Practice at the college's headquarters in Princes Gate, London, I suggested a day long conference on nutrition and health for which good speakers, whom I knew, would be invited. My request was greeted with total rejection, expressed with a tinge of ridicule that this temple of General Practice should be soiled by a discussion on food. Rejection of the dietary cause of ill health makes a mockery of the title "Health Service". Since the NHS started in 1948, mortality rates may have fallen due to lower infant mortality and the use of antibiotics, but postponement of death does not always bring health.

In the near 60 years of the NHS the nation has endured:

a) Coronary heart disease increasing in the 1950s to 'epidemic' proportions. b) a similar increase has occurred for diabetes and obesity. c) Increase in asthma, eczema, and hay fever. d) An overall increase in the incidence of cancer. e) Hospital infections which can kill.

It is, of course, beyond our wildest dreams, to suppose that any political party will dare to suggest the need to dismantle the NHS and to call it The National Medical Service. My plea is that the only way to secure adequate funding for hospitals and general practice is a system in which income is generated by payments made for items of service. Other European countries have achieved this without, apparently, denying care to the unemployed or other low income groups. Surely we are capable of learning how to combine state and private insurance so that standards, of which we can be proud, will match those of other nations.

REFERENCES

1. Bartholomew James, *The Welfare State We're In* pp 87-150 Methuen Publishing Ltd, London 2004
2. Corinthians 1, Ch.13.
3. Bartholomew James, *The Welfare State We're In* Chap. 3
4. *Amicitiae Memoir* Proceedings of 31st Jan. 1902 in honour of Dr. David Yellowlees, Printed for Private Circulation
5. Bartholomew James, *The Welfare Stat We're In, pp54-61*
6. McCarrison Sir R. *Nutrition and Health.* Wesbury Press, Brentwood 1982
7. Cleave T L, *The Saccharine Disease,* John Wright & Sons, Bristol 1974

CHAPTER 18
THE USES OF ADVERSITY 2

ALGERIA 1942/43

How long were we to hang about in the cold and rain of this God-forsaken railway siding, high in North Africa's Atlas mountains? As a Corps Field Ambulance we had been ordered to move forward in a mountain railway train, to prepare for the spring offensive by British, American and French army divisions against Rommel's Africa Corps; the objective, to defeat the enemy by joining up with Montgomery's 8th Army and to take Tunis and Bizerta, which would clear out the German forces from North Africa, was to be brilliantly achieved in May 1943. But meanwhile, long before signs of Spring, our Field Ambulance was making for a new base area near the town of Setif situated close to the Tunisian border and nearer the front line. Our carriages had been shunted into a siding in order to make way for supply trains, loaded with ammunition, to be used in the coming attack.

The cold, the rain, the boredom, and a rumour that German paratroops had dropped somewhere down the line were the least of my personal 'adversities'; pain in my right palm for several days had now developed into a full blown palmer space abscess. The signs and symptoms, typical of this infection – an acutely painful, throbbing hand, with swollen fingers looking like sausages – were now accompanied by shivering, fever, general malaise and pain running up to the swollen glands of my axilla (arm-pit).

AMMUNITION TRAIN

It was clear that the gathering abscess would have to be lanced without delay. In the medical world, Penicillin was still a mere distant rumour of a magic mould which killed bacteria; antibiotics had not yet arrived in Africa, and although our Field Ambulance had five RAMC officer doctors, we lacked premises and tools for a minor operation. So, assuming that a CCS (Casualty Clearing Station) or even an army hospital had been established in our corps base area near Setif, I sought permission from our colonel to beg a lift from the next ammunition train bound for that town.

The colonel, bleary eyed and shaky, fortifying himself against the cold by increasing his already high daily dose of Gin, agreed to my request. So when the next ammunition train stopped briefly, a friendly French engine driver welcomed me to the small cabin at the rear of his engine and suggested that he should, at the next stop, warn the Setif station master by telephone of the arrival of a casualty. After a full day's travel we arrived in the dark at Setif, where I bade farewell to the engine driver and was greeted by two young French men as I descended from the train, my arm in a sling. They escorted me to a rather battered old Citroen which proclaimed its purpose by a ragged Red Cross flag, tied to the car roof.

THE CASERNE

'*Hospital Anglais?*' I asked my escorts, '*Non, Non*', they replied, ' *Caserne.*' No British RAMC units were evidently yet established in the vicinity and soon, as the car drove through a kind of Foreign Legion Fort gate way, I was to learn that 'Caserne' meant barracks with an attached hospital wing. The car deposited me at the door leading to the medical reception room where Monsieur le Commandant, of the Corps Sanitaire, Francais, wearing a white woollen polo neck sweater, examined my hand; '*A ha!*' he exclaimed, '*fracture.*' In my broken French, I frantically tried to give the correct diagnosis; luckily, '*infection*' and '*abscess*' have much the same pronunciation in French, as in English, and to emphasise the required treatment I mimed, with my left index finger, the stroke of a scalpel blade on the spot between the third and fourth fingers where the abscess was obviously pointing. He looked again, said '*d'accord*' and with a gesture, invited me to get on to a primitive operating table.

FALSE HOPES

Is it a universal truth that, when anticipating some event or activity, the human imagination is always extremely over optimistic? I had envisaged an efficient RAMC anaesthetist putting me to sleep after an orderly had cleansed my hand and arm, so that an experienced surgeon would do the job of incising and draining. There might even be a smart QA nurse to cool my fevered brow! Alas for expectations! Here I was, dirty, fevered and afraid, as I watched the Commandant, having donned thick rubber gloves, rummage in a cabinet drawer for a scalpel which he dipped briefly in a dish of, presumably, surgical spirit.

'*Anaesthesie?*' said I, in rather a quivering voice. He seemed to treat this as an unnecessary suggestion, but the door opened and a lady appeared, draped in traditional Arab robes, barefooted with brass bangles round wrists and ankles; she smiled as she brandished a phial of ethyl chloride spray. Highly volatile ethyl chloride is used mostly as an inhaled general anaesthetic; it is sometimes sprayed on skin as a local anaesthetic; by evaporation, ethyl chloride could certainly freeze a small area of skin but it was useless for this particular operation, which I had been taught, always required a general anaesthetic.

INCISION

My outstretched hand was grasped and vaguely sprayed; I hope that never again will I have to experience pain of such shattering intensity. As the scalpel blade bit into inflamed tissues, searing, scalding agony ripped through my whole body; a glance at the scene of torment showed a gush of pus and blood around the blade still deep in the wound. After a dressing had been quickly applied, as in a nightmare, with blurred consciousness, I was aware of being helped up a flight of stairs to a small, two bedded room. For a few hours, postoperative pain-relief gave hope, but after two sleepless nights of renewed pain and misery the hand was, if anything worse; to my surprise a drain had not been inserted to keep the wound open, so in the absence of adequate drainage, the infection was still active.

When the commandant did his visiting round, on the third postoperative day, we agreed that the wound would have to be opened up under an "anasthesie general." Again I lay on the operating table and again the robed lady approached with the same ethyl chloride phial, but this time she also carried a standard open mask on which a piece of gauze or other cloth is fixed so that, when the mask is placed over a patient's face, vapour from liquid chloroform or other anaesthetic, applied drop by drop to the mask, is inhaled. Before I lost consciousness, I felt liquid anaesthetic cascading over my face.

After what seemed to be a long journey to a strange land of dreams, I became aware of peering faces and rather strident voices. On looking back, I wondered if, thanks to an over-dose of anaesthetic, a some point during the operation, I had stopped breathing. Back in the ward when an orderly came to change the dressing, the wound seemed certainly to have been opened up and drainage improved.

It was cheering at this juncture of my story to be joined by another British casualty, an officer of the Intelligence Corps, who had dislocated his right shoulder when his motor bicycle crashed on one of the approach roads to Setif which were occasionally being strafed by marauding Messerschmitt German fighter planes. The shoulder had been sorted, but between us we had only two left hands with which to assist our eating and fetching. No nurses or orderlies, it seemed, were now available for this part of the military hospital; an outbreak of typhus fever[2] among French North African troops had brought about the admission of many stricken soldiers to another wing of the hospital and had caused a staff shortage crisis.

The "Toilets" added to our misery; they were situated along the wall of a broad corridor, a row of three or four stalls, enclosed by low (about three feet high) partitions and doors; the familiar foot rests over a hole in the concrete floor made one-handed adjustment of one's trousers rather difficult. The world understands why populations, living in low rainfall countries which are not blessed with abundant water supplies, are denied the luxury of flushed water closets. But there is surely no need in such situations to dispense with a reasonable degree of privacy! Is it oversensitive to feel highly embarrassed on finding oneself squatting more or less in public and able to exchange greetings with the passing throng?

---

[2] Typhus fever can be spread by body lice; a serious, sometimes fatal fever, it has often plagued soldiers under conditions of war.

An Angel Came

A day or two after the second operation, the *precious jewel* of adversity or should I say an angel, appeared on the scene, in the form of an attractive young lady, the wife of a local Gendarme officer. She had trained as a nurse in Paris and had answered a call from the Caserne, for volunteer nurses to ease the staffing crisis. She took over the battle field of my right palm and came daily to change the dressing and to check that the wound continued to drain. I was relieved to see, by the way she handled instruments and dressings, that here was a high standard of nursing care; I owe this angel a debt of gratitude; thanks to her care, I sensed the dawn of recovery. It took about a fortnight for healing to progress to the point where the symptoms of infection spreading up my arm disappeared and I began to feel almost normal.

When the time came to say farewell to the Caserne, I departed through the arched entrance with my pack on my back and my arm still in a sling, wondering where to go. My fellow officers of the Field Ambulance had evidently not thought that it was worthwhile searching for me. As I watched the scene on this busy street, Arabs strolling and trading, or tending little charcoal fires for cooking things outside shop doors, the occasional donkey with a rider, mingling with passing British army trucks, I remembered hearing of soldiers in foreign lands who, from chance or design, became separated from their units. Rather than return to battle, so the story goes, they had merged into the countryside, got jobs, perhaps even married, a tale which is probably fiction and which I was not tempted to follow.

But the experience of being a patient so far from the customary surroundings, and emerging from a horrible world of pain and fever had lifted my thinking to unexpected realms. Except for the occasional British army truck, the street scene was almost biblical, so the memory of the assault on *one* of my hands, compelled thoughts of the agony of crucifixion in which *both* hands *and feet* were pierced not by a scalpel, but by nails; this led to the wonder of the first Easter and the certainty that, without the Crucifixion, there would have been no Resurrection, and without the Resurrection no Christianity.

ONLY FAIRY STORIES?

In Radio Four debates on Christianity, it is annoying to listen to Humanists and atheists, declaring in self-righteous tones, that they don't believe in biblical "Fairy Stories". The New Testament account, in John's Gospel, of the arrest, trial, and death by crucifixion of Jesus is no fairy story, it is a first hand account of the iniquity of officials using intrigue, cruelty and torture against an innocent victim. The first act of the drama begins with the apparent total destruction of the mission of Jesus. Thanks to the treachery of Judas, the arrest and trial of the Messiah took place late at night to avoid a hostile reaction by the crowds. All but two of the disciples, Peter and one other, fled when the soldiers and Jewish officials entered the garden of Gethsemane. After the bogus trials and, on the following day, and after the agonising death of Jesus on the cross, it seemed certain that all the Messianic hopes and dreams of his followers and friends had been shattered.

REMEMBER GAMALIEL

The above pattern of events seemed to be an example of the uprisings described in a speech to the Sanhedrin by Gamiliel, one of its Pharisee members, quoted in my chapter 9. Political/religious uprisings in Judaea, he declared, were not uncommon but after the capture and execution of the leaders, these movements invariably came to nothing.

It looked as if a similar outcome of the preaching of Jesus was now certain; after the events described above, all but two of the disciples had fled into hiding; Peter, after his initial boldness in drawing his sword, had broken down, weeping, in the courtyard of the chief priest's house, after denying thrice, that he had anything to do with his beloved master. So the end of the first Act of this real drama, sees the sorrowing group of friends and relatives watching, as Jesus dies on the cross; then comes the placing of the body in a tomb by Joseph of Arimathea, helped by Nicodemus (John Ch. 19: vv 38 – 42). In these verses, John states that because of fear of the Jews, Joseph had to keep secret his support of Jesus. Widespread fear of being exposed as a follower of Jesus tells of the enormity of the apparent defeat of the Messiah's mission.

THE EMPTY TOMB

But early in the first day of a new week everything changes. Mary Magdalene comes running to Peter with news of the empty tomb and soon the appearances of the risen Christ are real enough to convince even doubting Thomas of the truth of the Resurrection. There is no way, other than the Resurrection, to explain the transformation in the actions and morale of the disciples; from now on, defeat and despair turn in to joy. Peter and John, inspired by the Holy Spirit, are soon preaching in the Temple courts and boldly condemning those who killed Jesus; in Jesus' name they heal a crippled beggar and attract crowds of followers from far and wide who, in spite of frantic attempts of the Sanhedrin to stifle their movement, meet together in fellowship; in this way the Christian church is born. It cannot be stated often enough that, without the resurrection of Jesus, these things would not have happened.

John's narrative of this history, far from being a fairy tale, is full of intriguing historical details, written by a witness who was there. For instance, when Jesus was escorted, as a prisoner, to the house of Caiaphas, the High Priest, how could the other disciple, following the arrest party with Peter, be welcomed into the courtyard because he was 'known to the High Priest'? Scholars agree that the 'other disciple' was John, the writer of the fourth gospel, and son of the Galilean fisherman, Zebedee. So how could this young man from Galilee be known to the leader of the Jewish religious government and to the maid servant on duty who had no hesitation letting him into the court of the house and then agreeing to his request to let in Peter?

FISH FOR THE HIGH PRIEST

The most likely explanation, given by Professor Barclay (1), is as follows:

We know that Zebedee employed hired servants in his fishing boats, (Mark 1: 20) he must, therefore, have been the owner of a large fishing business. In the days before refrigeration was dreamed of, fish from the sea of Galilee had to be salted before being exported to the city of Jerusalem where, for many people, salted fish was their staple diet.

In one of the city's streets an Arab coffee house is situated on a site of a very early Christian church, said to have been built where stood a house, belonging to Zebedee. The Franciscan order of the Roman Catholic church believes that this original house on that site was a branch office of the Zedebee business. It is fair to suppose that the sons of Zebedee; James and John, were involved in the business and that John, in delivering fish to the High Priest's house, became well known to the household. The evidence may be slender but this theory does ring true in explaining an otherwise puzzling relationship.

Frank Morrison, who set out to research the truth of the Resurrection, has written one of the most fascinating accounts of the events of the first Easter, his book should be studied by those who scorn the New Testament as a 'Fairy Tale' (2).

An arm sling, like a white stick for the blind, often evokes sympathy; as I stood watching the life of that Algerian street in the spring of 1943, it was not long before the first military truck which I thumbed for a lift, immediately stopped and took me on my way to search for my Field Ambulance.

References

1. Barclay William, *The Gospel of John Vol 2,* p229, Saint Andrew Press, Edinburgh., 1955, revised 1975.
2. Morrison Frank, *Who Moved the Stone?* Faber Ltd 1930, Reprinted by OM Publishing, 1983, 2001

CHAPTER 19
SIMPLE EXPLANATIONS

'Nearly 2500 years ago the Greeks had already realised that one of the most important of empirical facts is that correct explanations are nearly always simple explanations'. (1)

I read somewhere, that after publishing their first book, writers often feel compelled to start, at once, on another. That certainly was how I reacted when my book, *A Doctor in the Wilderness,* at last appeared in 1993, as a 'Vanity' publication; none of the conventional publishers, who had been approached, wanted to take it on, so, in the belief that the book's message was important, I paid for the cost of production and was gratified when the steady sale of the first thousand copies and a sustained demand, requiring a second printing in 1995, meant that I would not be out of pocket.

I did not write to make money but hoped that the book might persuade both doctors and consumers that the dreadfully high level of bodily ill-health, particularly in Scotland, was due, above all, to a simple nutritional cause. This truth did not stem from the dreams of theorists; research by distinguished scientists in many countries had proved beyond doubt the vital importance of sound nutrition as the basis of health. The disturbing increase in the UK during the 20th century of crimes and offences bear a striking resemblance to the graphs illustrating the increase of certain bodily diseases during the same period. Some of my respected colleagues in the field of nutrition research suggest that *both criminal behaviour and bodily disease are caused by the same faulty nutrition.* The researches of the following four scientists certainly seem to give some support to the belief that processed food and drink can adversely effect mental health.

NUTRITION AND PHYSICAL DEGENERATION

The American dentist Weston Price, in a worldwide investigation, found that during pregnancy, if a mother's diet consisted of unnatural, processed foods, bereft of adequate vitamins, minerals and other essential nutrients, her baby might suffer from abnormal skull formation, cleft palate, deformed dental arches and other congenital faults; according to Price, those of the skull can lead to defective brain development and to a tendency to criminal behaviour. He recorded that isolated peoples living off 'natural' foods had no need, in their crime-free populations, for prisons; he also classed as 'unnatural,' foods grown on soils depleted by modern agriculture.(2)

McCarrison's Rats

In one of his classic feeding trials Sir Robert McCarrison compared the health of a colony of young laboratory rats, eating a defective dietary regime, as consumed by low-income English people, with the performance of a rat colony eating a diet similar to that of the Sikhs and Hunzas in northern India. The *'poor Class'* English diet *'consisted of white bread, margarine, over-sweetened tea with a little milk, (of which the rats consumed large quantities) boiled cabbage and boiled potato, tinned meat and tinned jam of the cheaper sort'.*

The contrasting Sikh diet featured whole grain cereals, milk and milk products, legumes, green leaf vegetables and fresh fruits.

The members of the well fed group *'lived happily together, they increased in weight and flourished. The other group did not increase in weight; their growth was stunted.......they were nervous and apt to bite the attendants; they lived unhappily together and by the sixtieth day of the experiment they began to kill and eat the weaker ones amongst them. When they had disposed of three in this way I was compelled to segregate the remainder.'* Note that the malnourished rats had as much food as they wished; they were not starved (3).

Disturbed Children

Dr. Ian C. Menzies, former Consultant Psychiatrist of Tayside Health Board Young Person's Psychiatric Unit, in the 1980s studied the recent apparent increase in the problems posed by children, displaying disruptive and aggressive behaviour, who did not respond to psychiatric therapy. In some cases, the severity of the continuing hostile violence of these children made their family life a veritable hell on earth (4).

The cases described by Dr. Menzies demonstrated dramatic relief when '*Sweets or drinks containing additives, especially colourings*' were excluded from the diet of the disturbed children. He quotes from an author who believes that sucrose (refined sugar) *'may act in some unknown way synergistically with additives.'* (synergistically means enhancing the harmful effect of the additives). He also referred to scientists in Germany who claimed that a common additive, phosphoric acid, used to stabilise carbonated (fizzy) soft drinks contributed to hyperactivity and violence in children. A survey in the US, of delinquent and disorderly children, found that they were drinking per head, annually, between 1,215 and 1,500 cans of carbonated soft drinks. (4)

THE LATE DR. RICHARD MACKARNESS

In 1974 during a postgraduate study of nutrition, I had the privilege of visiting the Rooksdown Hospital, Park Prewet, Basingstoke where the late Dr.Mackarness, working as an associate specialist in psychiatry, pioneered his unique Clinical Ecology Unit. His drive in this venture came from his own personal experience of illness being cured by a US doctor, Theron Randolf , Director of the Chicago Ecology Unit.

In his two books *Not All in the Mind,* and *Chemical Victims,* Dr. Mackarness gives a fascinating account of his success in treating patients, diagnosed as cases of chronic mental illness whose symptoms were, in truth, due to food or chemical allergy. His proposal to set up a Clinical Ecology Unit at Rooksdown Hospital met with intense hostility and opposition from his psychiatric colleagues who declared that the allergy theory was a load of rubbish.

The hospital authorities may well have been swayed to support Dr. Mackarness' project by the case of a lovely young woman who suffered from severe depression and bouts of terrible violence; psychiatrists had advised leucotomy, but Dr. Mackarness pled to be allowed use his diagnostic method whereby the patient is tested for reactions to various foods or drinks. In the case of the young women, the tests revealed outbursts of violence in response to some foods, particularly, to instant coffee, of which she had been drinking vast quantities. Withdrawal of the guilty substances restored her sanity and saved her from the dreaded leucotomy.

INCREASING ALLERGY

The work of Dr. Richard Mackerness, possibly more than that of any other UK doctor, laid the foundations of the growing interest, among doctors and their patients, in research on food intolerance and allergy. There is no doubt that in recent decades, illnesses, such as asthma, eczema and hay fever, have greatly increased and have given birth to variously named societies, AAA (Action Against Allergy) and more recently, to BSEM (British Society for Ecological Medicine). Some organic enthusiasts suggest that allergies might not occur if guilty foods were grown organically, but I know of no scientific proof that this is true.

The reaction of the psychiatric consultant staff of Rooksdown Hospital to Dr. Mackarness reminds us of the exasperation, expressed by the 18th century naval surgeon, James Lind, who was ridiculed by the doctors of his day when he demonstrated that a simple remedy, consumption of citrus fruits, could cure and prevent scurvy; a similar case was that of Ignaz Semmelwiess when, in 1847 his colleagues in Vienna poured scorn on his demonstration that hand washing by attendants, before assisting at childbirth, would prevent the often fatal disease, maternal puerperal fever. Simplicity in causation seemed, to those academics, to be beyond belief.

If allergic reaction to food or food additives is a significant cause of criminal behaviour, it is important to ask the following question: suppose that, by some massive dietary reformation, our nation's larders had been filled with additive-free, unrefined, unprocessed organically grown, fresh food, would we all, like McCarrison's rats, be 'living happily together' in a land where there was no need for prisons? The evidence of Weston Price, quoted above, might suggest a positive reply. But it is necessary to be reminded that the message of a well known story would not agree that Utopia could come through perfect nutrition.

A STORY OF CRIME

The story cannot be classed as scientific evidence but it does illustrate a deep truth on human behaviour; here it is:

A family of father, mother, and two sons depended for their nourishment on a diet which could hardly have shown a greater contrast from the ..*tinned meat, white bread and margarine, boiled cabbage and sweetened tea etc.* which had such a disastrous effect on McCarrison's rats. The family used the food harvested from their splendid garden; various fruit trees ensured a good supply of fresh fruits. However, unlike the laboratory rats eating a Sikh diet, the family, alas, did not '*live happily together*'. Sibling jealousy led to violent behaviour: '*Cain said to his brother Abel, "Let us go out to the field" And while they were in the field, Cain attacked his brother Abel and killed him' (Genesis 4:8).* Cain had lured his brother into the field, so the murder was premeditated.

SUMMING UP

The evidence from the above four examples of published research, demonstrating a link between faulty nutrition and abnormal mental states, is strong and cannot be dismissed, but the story of 'Cain and Abel tells us that, unfortunately, human beings however well they are nourished, may still be driven by impulses of jealousy, aggression and hate. To most Christians, on this side of the Atlantic, the Genesis story of creation is not history and, as suggested in chapter 7, the account of the Garden of Eden need not clash with Darwin's theory of evolution; but it does give a profound insight into our relationships with each other, and with our Creator; it also teaches that we must work if we are to eat.

Unlike animals we were given knowledge of good and evil and since the fall of Adam and Eve, we know that there is such a thing as sin which can be elaborated under the seven headings: Pride, Envy, Anger, Sloth, Avarice, Gluttony, and Lust. Does nutrition have anything to do with the seven virtues with which we can confront our sins: Wisdom, Justice, Courage Temperance, Faith, Love, and Hope?(5)

In trying to answer that question and to sum up this controversy in the simplest possible language, we can conclude: yes, there is evidence that diet can influence mental activity but, in the making of either criminals or saints, much deeper influences surely come from family background, social environment, education and above all, religious belief. *A Time to Weep* attempts to show that the catastrophic decline in our nation's standard of morality, particularly since the end of World War 2, is due to a simple cause – the nationwide loss of our Christian faith, a faith which teaches that the family of one wife and one husband, seeking to live according to the teaching of Christ and the guidance of the Bible, with its Ten Commandments, is the foundation of a stable, civilised society.

Professor William Barclay's clear advice is worth repeating: *'Those who wish to enjoy the privileges of a Christian civilisation ought to ask themselves if they are doing anything to keep the civilisation Christian; and if they are not, they will have no one but themselves to blame if they wake up one day and find their privileges gone.'*

It was encouraging to receive letters from several readers of *A Doctor in the Wilderness* who thanked me for what I had written. But if A Time to Weep ever finds a publisher, will the book be written off as the havering of a senile old doctor who has no right to meddle in or to pontificate on religious matters? My reply is that, in general practice, about one third of patients, complaining of distress, pain or general malaise, are presenting symptoms which are not of physical, but of emotional origin, the latter caused almost invariably by broken human relationships. (When, of course, the possibility of food allergy has been excluded !)

'THE WORLD'S A STAGE'

Thus, the listening GP ... *'is rewarded by a glimpse into the vast underworld of the dynamics of human emotion, a world of ever continuing drama, how profoundly true then, that "All the world's a stage and all the men and women merely players."* (6)

...We, in general practice, have the best view of this kind of stage; as our patients act out their little dramas we are frequently called on to the stage to play a part, sometimes we are even invited backstage where we see the players without their make up and without their masks...

Over the last decade, membership of the Church of Scotland has fallen by 85,766. Whether the statistics of trends in divorce, crime and church membership have any significance in relation to psychiatric illness, I do not know, but I am quite sure that on a personal level the amount of neurotic illness will always depend on the integrity of the biological unit of society, the family.

On the stage of Christendom, in seeking guidance to problems of personal and national life, the people traditionally put at the centre of their stage, the man of God, the preacher. Even if both preacher and audience often failed down the centuries to live up to the message that was preached, nonetheless in all walks of life, formal recognition was given to an optimistic Divine purpose, and to the active presence of the devil. But over the last 200 years the audience has become increasingly bored with this kind of sermon, and one reason for their distraction has been the dramatic entry of a flamboyant character, the Wizard. In the 'Dramatis Personae' of this fantasia the Wizard is described as a "technocrat or technologist who believes in salvation through scientific and industrial advancement: despises the Preacher". ...the Wizard deserves the thunderous applause he has been given as Act follows Act, moon rockets and monoamin oxidase inhibitors, atomic fission and television, jet propulsion and juke boxes, computers and contraceptive pills... he (the Wizard) has become so pleased with himself – he knows not the meaning of the word humility and is a chap of endless conceit – that he has pushed the preacher into the wings, mounted the pulpit and started preaching sermons his elevation there is a dangerous thing.. because his sermon is based on the rather nebulous Freudian doctrine that the chief end of man is the pursuit of personal wealth and pleasure and touches not at all on the inescapable knowledge of good and evil...'
(7)

THE END OF THE ROAD

In 1995, as I began to create A Time to Weep, the going was getting a bit rough; a hip replacement in 1996 did not help creative writing, nor did moving house in 1998 when all books, files, journals and documents had to be re-located. By 2003, the Introduction and first chapters had taken shape but in June of that year came the shattering blow, from which full recovery is impossible; after a short illness my dear wife, Sonia, died. We had been together for 53 years. How strange that shortly after I had chosen my book's title, here was the ultimate, terrible time for weeping. In the desolation of being alone, the urge to continue writing came, somehow, as a kind of therapy, but by then, in my mid eighties, I wondered, would I be spared to finish the job? My only trace of comfort lay in the thought that it was kinder, for my wife not to be the one who was left alone.

I did not know how to end this chapter until I remembered the help given by two of my stalwart friends. The first is Dr Bill Abel, retired consultant psychiatrist and devout Christian, whose wife died about a month before the death of Sonia. During discussions on our predicament his total belief on the certainty of a great reunion is comforting, however difficult for our earthly minds to comprehend.

The second helper is Jock Scott-Park, an organic dairy farmer, skiing companion on the rugged slopes of Scotland's Glen Coe, and on two memorable occasions on the kinder ski runs of the Andorran, Pyrenees mountains. A few weeks ago, almost as if, by some mysterious telepathy he was aware of my reference to Bill Abel's conviction on re-union, Jock sent to me the following moving poem by an unknown author:

> As the faint dawn crept upward, grey and dim,
> He saw her move across the past to him,
> Her eyes as they had looked in long-gone years,
> Tender with love, and soft with thoughts of tears,
> Her hands outstretched as if in wonderment,
> Nestled in his and rested there content.
> "Dear wife" he whispered, "what glad dream is this?
> I feel your clasp – your long – remembered kiss
> Touches my lips as when you used to creep
> Into my heart; and yet, this is not sleep –
> Is it some vision, that with night will fly?"
> "Nay, dear" she answered; "it is really I"

"Dear heart, it is you, I know
But I knew not the dead could meet us so,
Bodied as we are – see how like we stand!"
"Like," she replied "in form and face and hand"
Silent awhile, he held her to his breast,
As if afraid to try the further test –
Then speaking quickly, "Must you go away?"
"Husband," she murmured, "neither night nor day!"
Close to her then she drew his head,
Trembling, "I do not understand", he said,
"I thought the spirit world was far apart" —
"Nay" she replied, "it is not now, dear heart !
Quick, hold fast my hand, lean on me …so…
Cling to me, dear…..'tis but a step to go
The white-faced watchers rose, beside the bed
"Shut out the day," they sighed, "our friend is dead."(8)

Any words with which a tearful author might seek to follow the deeply moving thoughts of that unknown poet would be superfluous. We can only pray for the certainty of the promise that awaits us – *A Time*, not *to Weep*, but *A Time to Rejoice*.

REFERENCES

1. Cleave TL *The Saccharine Disease p iv John Wrigth & Son Bristol 1974*
2. Price Weston A, *Nutrition and Physical Degeneration,* Published by the Author, Redlands California 1939.
3. McCarrison R *Nutrition and Health* p29. First Published by Faber and Faber Ltd, London. New edition published in 1982 by the McCarrison Society, Printed by The Westbury Press.
4. Menzies Ian C. *Disturbed Children The Role of Food and Chemical Sensitivities..* Nutrition and Health 1984, vol 3,
5. Olsson K.A. *Seven Sins and Seven Virtues, Hodder and Stoughton 1959, 1962.*
6. Shakespeare *As you Like it, Act ii, sc. 7,*
7. Yellowlees W. *All the World's a Stage,* J.RCGP, Supplement No.3, Vol XV11(No.82) pp30-35Randall E *The Dead have never Died.* George Allen & Unwin London 1918

EPILOGUE

But how the subject-theme may gang,
Let time and chance determine;
Perhaps it may turn out a sang;
Perhaps turn out a sermon.

(Burns; Epistle to a young friend May 1786)

My Introduction featured a poem on *Old Age* by the anonymous author of the Bible's book of Ecclesiastes; it seemed fitting, therefore, that an epilogue should open with the above stanza from a poem by Robert Burns to a *Young Friend*. Burns was evidently unsure whether his advice, from age to youth, would turn out to be a song or a sermon. It reads as if the latter prevailed and although the biblical writer and the Ayrshire farmer were separated, in time, by over two thousand years, they both seem to agree that the following brief summing up, might well suffice for the epilogue of *A Time to Weep*: *here is the conclusion of the matter. Fear God and keep his commandments, for this is the whole duty of man.* (Ecclesiastes, 12: 13)

In writing *A Time to Weep*, my endeavour was to show what happens when a nation fails, sadly, in its 'whole duty'; readers can decide whether I have created a song or a sermon. As told in the last chapter, the title and the opening pages were written before the sudden death of my dear wife, Sonia, brought a terrible, agonising 'Time to Weep'. To continue writing then became a kind of therapy against loneliness and grief.

TIME AND CHANCE

Do the vagaries of 'Time and Chance' which helped Burns to create the verses of his *Epistle to a Young Friend*, come to the rescue of other writers? I experienced an example of this process on 25th January 2008 (Burns night).

Various demands on my time left me sitting down wearily at the end of a busy day, wondering if I could muster sufficient energy to compose an acceptable epilogue for *A Time to Weep*. 'By Chance' I had noticed that BBC 2 proposed to do a TV programme on the life of the Scottish Bard; I could not resist the temptation to abandon the computer keyboard for the TV screen.

It would take many chapters to write a full review of the ethical standards now prevailing in radio and TV. We elderly widowers, in our loneliness may well seek solace by listening to radio or watching admirable TV documentaries on history, wildlife, sport and so on; but many of my fellow 'oldies' agree that programmes, which are supposed to entertain, with a few notable exceptions, can truly be classed as drivel, often expressed in foul language, laced with violence and explicit sex. Such programmes stray far from St. Paul's advice to the Philippians:

Whatever is true, whatever is noble, whatever is right, whatever is pure whatever is lovely...think about such things.

MEDIAWATCH-UK

How much of the rise in crime, family breakdown and lawlessness in the second half of the 20th century has stemmed from the constant TV visual barrage of violence, sex, infidelity and murder? Some scientists who tell us that television has no effect on the behaviour of children or adolescents are contradicted by the following quotation, published in the Mediawatch-uk Booklet, *Children and the Media, Learning by example?:The average British 3 year–old is glued to a TV or computer screen for nearly 5 hours a day and almost half of all three-year-olds have a TV in their bedroom. Suddenly the outside world is coming into these children's lives...Most scientists now think that TV can encourage violent tendencies.*(1)

The Burns TV programme, mentioned above, deserves a place in this epilogue as a good example of the dismal decline in media standards, reflecting the depravity of modern culture in Britain and the destruction of our Christian heritage: viewers of the programme received scant reference to Burns' superb mastery both of the English language and of the lowland Scots dialect. We were given the briefest mention of his triumphant visits, following the publication of his poems, to Edinburgh, the Scottish Borders and to the Highlands; we were not told of the extraordinary acclaim showered on this poverty stricken farmer who could hold his own, not only among his Ayrshire cronies, but also, in the company of aristocratic land owners and scholars. Nor was there mention of his rash political gesture when, in 1782, he purchased four cannons costing £3 to be sent to the rebels of the French Revolution.

No, we were told of none of these things; instead, a leering female presenter, with many a facial smirk, revelled in references to poet's promiscuity. On that evening, I longed to protest to the BBC.

Here again, *time* and *chance* came to my rescue; yesterday evening (17/03/08). I was privileged to hear an eloquent lecture, delivered in Aberfeldy by Mrs Pauline Webborn, an assistant of John Beyer, the Director of Mediawatch-uk. In vivid language she told us of media corruption and wickedness, of how the spread of the Internet and use of sophisticated mobile phones give children and adolescents access to vile pornographic images.

' To Weep' is a poor response to this dreadful corruption of our children; 'A Time for Action' is urgently required; our thanks are due to Mediawatch-uk for advice on how to protest, advice which I felt bound to follow having watched, on 23rd March, (Easter Sunday) the BBC's *The Passion,* a programme supposed to depict the events of the Crucifixion and Resurrection of our Lord.

The warped minds of BBC producers managed to transform the lucid biblical account of the arrest, trial, crucifixion, and resurrection of Jesus into a muddled travesty of the truth. Joseph of Arimathea was presented as a small dark-skinned man, wearing a turban, whose conversation was totally unclear; was he supposed to be a Muslim presence? If he was, the BBC's grasp of history was as faulty as their biblical presentation. Even worse, was the scene at the empty tomb, where an hysterical Mary Magdalene was seen repeatedly scraping up dust from the ground and hurling it at the tomb. The BBC spokesman to whom I complained about the absurdities of this programme seemed reluctantly to agree that I had a point; he muttered something about having to satisfy viewers; evidently, in this matter, biblical truth has little chance of survival in the hands of muddled, ignorant TV producers.

To readers who deplore that my *Time and Chance* have hatched an epilogue devoid of optimism I respond in the words of a writer who faced spiritual problems every bit as depressing as those we face in 21st century Britain today:

We wrestle not with flesh and blood but against powers and against authorities, against the world rulers of this darkness, against malicious spiritual forces in heavenly places. Because of this you must take the armour of God that you may be able to stand against them in the evil day.(2)

REFERENCES

1. *Children and the Media,* 2007, Mediawatch-UK. Printed in England by EAM Printers 01473 250291
2. *Barclay William.* The Daily Study Bible, pp181-183 Ephesians 6:10-20: according to Barclay, Paul wrote this letter in prison where he was chained by the wrist to an armed Roman soldier.

210